Front cover:
Anny Ondra as Alice White in Hitchcock's version of *Blackmail* (BIP, 1929).
(page 323)

This issue:
Screenwriters and screenwriting

Edited by John Belton

Editorial office:

Richard Koszarski
Box Ten
Teaneck, New Jersey, 07666, USA
E-mail: filmhist@aol.com

Publishing office:

John Libbey & Company Pty Ltd
Level 10, 15–17 Young Street
Sydney, NSW 2000
Australia
Telephone: +61 (0)2 9251 4099
Fax: +61 (0)2 9251 4428
E-mail: jlsydney@mpx.com.au

© 1997 John Libbey & Company Pty Ltd

Other offices:

John Libbey & Company Ltd
13 Smiths Yard, Summerley Street
London SW18 4HR, UK
Telephone: +44 (0)181-947 2777
Fax: +44 (0)1-947 2664

John Libbey Eurotext Ltd, Montrouge, France
John Libbey - CIC s.r.l., Rome, Italy

Printed in Australia by
Gillingham Printers Pty Ltd, South Australia

FI[LM]
HI[STORY]

CW00496063

An International Journal

Volume 9, Number 3, 1997

This issue: **SCREENWRITERS AND SCREENWRITING**

Film History, Volume 9, pp. 226–227, 1997. Copyright © John Libbey & Company
ISSN: 0892-2160. Printed in Australia

Screenwriters and screenwriting

Revisionist film historiography differs from traditional paradigms for the writing of film history in its attempt to understand the cinema as a 'system' and to identify the various practices that define this system. Thus David Bordwell, Janet Staiger, and Kristin Thompson, in their Classical Hollywood Cinema: Film Style & Mode of Production to 1960 (New York: Columbia University Press, 1985), view Hollywood cinema as a style of filmmaking shared by a large group of filmmakers. This group style or system consists of a norm of stylistic practices that evolved over the first twenty years of filmmaking in the United States. Subsequent histories of early cinema by Charles Musser, Eileen Bowser, Richard Koszarski, and others (see Scribners' History of the American Cinema series) concentrated less on individual films and filmmakers than on various practices, ranging from pre-existing entertainment practices, such as vaudeville, cartoon strips and popular songs, to various production, distribution, and exhibition practices.

However, revisionist historians have yet to write a history of screenwriting practices. Work has been done on individual screenwriters (see the review of Cari Beauchamp's book on Frances Marion in this issue or Pat McGilligan's series of Backstory books, containing interviews with individual screenwriters). This issue of Film History is a call for such a history.

Edward Azlant is the author of a pioneering study on screenwriting in silent American cinema. The article presented here, excerpted from his 1980 University of Wisconsin at Madison dissertation, provides a valuable map of American screenwriting prior to 1911. In it, he reviews the contribution of early story editors and screenwriters, and traces the relationship of the scenario to major industrial changes, such as the rise of the nickelodeon and the advent of the star system. Azlant's bibliography will hopefully provide readers with a starting place for their own research into screenwriting practices.

Isabelle Raynauld, who, since 1985, has been researching the history of the scenario in France prior to World War I, explores various types of scripts submitted for copyright purposes at the Arsenal Library. Her study, originally published in French in 1995 and translated here for an English-speaking audience, reveals the existence of hundreds of pre-war scripts, which were used as shooting scripts and which contained story-telling features that shed 'light on the way the decoupage developed and was planned' during the writing of the script.

This issue of Film History also contains a 'sampler' of articles on early screenwriting published in the Moving Picture World. Written by screenwriters Epes Winthrop Sargent, Jeanie Macpherson, and Lloyd Lonergan, these pieces outline the history of early screenwriting and suggest how screenwriting practices changed in the pre-war period.

Screenwriting practices can be documented and studied by looking at various manuals written for aspiring screenwriters. One of the most successful of such manuals became the basis for a popular correspondence school course in screenwriting, The Palmer Plan Handbook. Anne Morey discusses the history of the Palmer Photoplay Corporation and examines its attempts to streamline the process of photoplay construction, to mass produce screenwriters, and to educate its students to become 'better audiences'.

Patrick Loughney draws on written materials deposited at the Library of Congress to examine the range of different texts used by early motion picture producers to establish copyright over their films. He charts changes in these texts between 1895 (*Rip Van Winkle*) and 1912 (*From the Manager to the Cross*) which reflect the evolving function of the screenplay from a document that identifies the text as property for copyright purposes to streamlining production procedures. In an appendix, he presents samples of early scenarios as well as an exchange of letters that gives a sense of the emergence of the scenario as a work in itself.

In the essay on Charles Bennett, I attempt to trace certain story types found in Alfred Hitchcock's British films back to thematic and narrative interests that inform the dramatic works of one of the director's favourite screenwriting collaborators. The evolution of the 'typical' Hitchcock scenario during the early 1930s can be seen as the result of Hitchcock's productive partnership with Bennett.

A few weeks before this issue went to press, the University of Udine in Italy hosted an international conference on intertitles in silent cinema. As more and more scholars of early cinema begin to investigate screenwriting, intertitles and other story-telling features, the much-needed history of screenwriting practices called for in this issue will hopefully begin to take shape. We eagerly look forward to that.

I would like to thank the following individuals for their assistance in the preparation of this issue: Joanne Bernardi, Peter DeCherney, Richard Koszarski, Antonia Lant, Patrick Loughney, Janet Staiger, Tony Slide and Yuri Tsivian. ♠

John Belton, Associate Editor

UPCOMING ISSUES/ CALL FOR PAPERS

Film History 9, 4
International Cinema of the Teens
    edited by Kristin Thompson

Film History 10, 1
Cinema Pioneers
    edited by Stephen Bottomore
    (deadline for submissions
    1 September 1997)

Film History 10, 2
Film, Photography and Television
    edited by Richard Koszarski
    (deadline for submissions
    1 December 1997)

Film History 10, 3
Red Scare
    edited by Daniel J. Leab
    (deadline for submissions
    1 March 1998)

Film History 10, 4
Special issue on the Centennial of Cinema Literature.

Film History 11, 1
Film Technology
    edited by John Belton
    (deadline for submissions
    1 September 1998)

The editors of *FILM HISTORY* encourage the submission of manuscripts within the overall scope of the journal. These may correspond to the announced themes of future issues above, but may equally be on any topic relevant to film history.

Film History, Volume 9, pp. 228–256, 1997. Copyright © John Libbey & Company
ISSN: 0892-2160. Printed in Australia

Screenwriting for the early silent film: forgotten pioneers, 1897–1911

Edward Azlant

When the cinema began, no such danger [of a series of creative blood-lettings] existed – because no scenarios existed. Those primitive one and two-reelers were shot in a couple of days by directors who had a rough idea of the story and who improvised as they went along.

Kevin Brownlow[1]

Ince ... is credited with the introduction of the film scenario.

David Robinson[2]

The attitudes of the two film historians quoted above reflect widely held views of the role of screenwriting in the earliest era of film production. Brownlow observes that 'off-the-cuff' directorial invention characterised film's earliest days and continued well into the 1920s. Robinson recounts the common view that written design did not become normal practice until the early 1910s, largely under the supervision of Thomas Ince. Both views serve to obscure a rich and vital period of screenwriting, which attends the earliest developments of the motion picture.[3]

Early screenwriting can be traced back to pioneering efforts in narrative design. The process of design assumes an intermediate step between the materials used in an enterprise and the actual techniques of execution or production. This stage is normally a conceptual or planning phase, in which choices of materials are made, a preliminary outline of significant features is composed, and an underlying scheme governing the whole development or function of the creation is assigned or recognised.[4] Given this general sense of design, it is fitting to pursue the origins of the screenplay through film's evolving complexities of materials, features, schemes of development, and production circumstances, and through the backgrounds, attitudes, and activities of the artists attending this evolution.

The design of narrative art, to be enacted in a dramatic form, is an old practice. Thus, early screenwriting borrows much in concept, practice, personnel and instruction from the theatre, as well as from literature, the graphic arts, vaudeville and, most notably, journalism. Indeed, in his discussion of screen practices, Charles Musser traces the cinema back to early representational forms such as lantern slide shows, political cartoons, comic strips, fairy

Edward Azlant teaches film history and screenwriting at De Anza College and is a member of the Writers Guild of America. Correspondence should be addressed to Edward Azlant, c/o Film/TV, De Anza College, 21250 Stevens Creek Blvd., Cupertino, CA 95014, USA.

tales, illustrated lectures, newspaper stories, popular songs, vaudeville, and the theatre.[5] These other media clearly provide 'scenarios' of a sort for early motion pictures.

Design for the earliest films

The 'scenario' is a term probably derived from the name of the skeletal plot outline used in the *commedia dell'arte*. The first scenarios were probably not actual screenplays but rather skeletal outlines used in pre-production design. A careful analysis of early Lumière films (usually considered 'actualities') indicates a manifest sense of orderly process or consequential activity, suggesting a pre-production sense of structure.[6] Further, regarding the actual practice of pre-production design for that earliest of comic gag films, *L'Arroseur arrose* (1895), Louis Lumière recalled, 'I think I may say that the idea of the scenario was suggested to me by a farce by my brother Edouard.'[7]

One notably concrete instance of design occurred in 1897. During an early spate of filmed prizefights, Sigmund Lubin of Philadelphia produced a 'counterpart' of the Enoch Rector/Veriscope Company's mammoth 11,000-foot 'authentic' film of the Corbett–Fitzsimmons heavyweight championship fight recorded in Carson City, Nevada. Lubin employed two local stevedores to re-enact the fight in Philadelphia, on instruction from a 'director', who prompted the fighters from a round-by-round newspaper account of the actual fight.

There were a number of similarly bogus fight films produced in this period along with other films of re-enacted events and, as historian Terry Ramsaye has suggested, the newspaper account of the Corbett–Fitzsimmons fight used by Lubin's 'director' clearly served as an unintentional proto-scenario.[8]

This newspaper summary contained a skeletal description of consequential dramatic actions, segmented by units (i.e. round one) and marked by significant features (i.e. left jab by Fitzsimmons).

Thus, the combination of boxing and journalism might have helped film in realising its primary technique of design in creating 'counterpart' activities, which are at the heart of any fiction.

In 1897, W.B. Hurd of the American branch of the Lumière interests acquired the rights to film a folk presentation of the traditional Oberammergau *Passion Play* annually re-enacted in Bohemia. Hurd approached Rich G. Hollaman, a pioneer film exhibitor at the Eden Musee in New York, with the project, budgeted at $10,000 for film rights (a notable purchase), and an equal amount for production. Hollaman wavered, and Hurd sold the project to the theatrical producers Klaw and Erlanger. The film was produced, but the results were unimpressive in the eyes of Hollaman, who then initiated his own version from the ashes of a previous theatrical disaster.[9]

Two decades earlier, Salmi Morse, an eccentric California dramatist, had written his own spectacular version of the *Passion Play*, which was staged by impresario David Belasco at the Grand Opera House in San Francisco on 3 March 1879. Morse's drama, as produced by Belasco, consisted of a series of dialogues accompanied by pictures and tableaux. However, according to historian A. Nicholas Vardac:

> [T]he dialogue, it seems, was of minor importance, since the story of the events leading up to the Crucifixion and the Resurrection was told by the sequence of stage pictures ... The story and its drama was planned entirely from the visual point of view.[10]

Further, Vardac considers this production exemplary of the realistically visual or 'photographic' spectacle of the late nineteenth-century melodramatic stage.

In 1880, Morse, well on in years, came to New York hoping to see his version of the *Passion Play* produced. He acquired the financial backing of the noted theatrical producer Henry E. Abbey and costumer Albert G. Eaves. The play was lavishly mounted and rehearsed at an old church and its adjoining property, and was then banned before it opened by the mayor of New York on 'religious' grounds.

Morse was crushed and disappeared into poverty; he later committed suicide. However, when in 1897 Hollaman decided to produce his own film version of the *Passion Play*, he recalled Morse's cancelled production. Ramsaye astutely observes:

> Salmi Morse's ill-fated script was brought to light, to become the first [sic] motion picture

scenario. Hollaman induced Albert G. Eaves [who still had the costumes for the cancelled production] to join in a project to produce the *Passion Play* in New York, to be a *synthetic equivalent to the imported film*.[11] [emphasis added]

Hollaman's 'equivalent' version was shot on the roof of the Grand Central Palace. According to Ramsaye, the completed film (a lengthy 2100 feet in an era of 50-foot films without continuity titles or leaders but supported by a live lecturer and a boys choir), premiered at the Eden Musee on 30 January 1898. It was initially advertised as an authentic record of the Bohemian ritual, but the ruse was soon exposed by the New York *Herald*. Surprisingly, the discovery of fabrication apparently had no ill effects on attendance, and Hollaman's film enjoyed a great commercial success, which Ramsaye attributes to its 'pictorial superiority' over the 'actual' but unpopular Klaw and Erlanger version. Ramsaye roots this superiority in a sense of dramatic construction, ostensibly engineered by actor Frank Russell, who played 'Christus', and cameraman William C. Paley, both in league against director L.J. Vincent, who suffered the delusion he was making still-lantern slides for stereoptic presentation. It is much more probable that this sense of dramatic construction was promoted by Morse's highly visual manuscript. A contemporary observer, an anonymous scenario editor (most probably Lee Dougherty of Biograph) writing in *Photoplay* magazine in 1914, recalled his reaction to the Hollaman film:

> The pictures shown at the Eden Musee ... were nearly all scenes of raging seas, trains in motion, waterfalls and the like. But the *Passion Play* was different. I got to thinking 'some one must have written that story or put it into some form for picture production', but no one could tell me more than I already knew myself.[12]

The productions of the 'counterpart' fight film and the 'equivalent' *Passion Play* suggest that the filming of fabricated, dramatic events naturally required pre-production design. The evolving complexities of film materials, such as distinct characters or multiple settings, and of film production, as manifest by the extraordinary length of these primitive films, demanded a certain attention to pre-production design.

Generally, our view of film history around the turn of the century remains murky and yet, by most accounts, projected motion pictures lost some of their public novelty around 1898. Film producers responded to this slackening of interest by making qualitative changes in their motion pictures over the next half-decade, mainly involving longer and different types of films. Film length grew from the earliest standard of 50 feet to a 250– to 400– foot range by 1900, and further to 300 to 600 feet by 1903. Film content shifted from novel and ingenious incidents and events to 'prearranged scenes', in the forms of playlets or storyettes of chases, simple comedies, magical or 'mysterious' presentations, episodic action tableaux and filmed theatricals.[13] Whatever the form, the two constants in this period of the emergence of narrative film were increased length and some manifestation of design or prearrangement. This transition clearly involves the craft of screenwriting, a practice that could be fairly described as the pre-arrangement of scenes.

Roy L. McCardell

In 1898, the Biograph studio designated film writing as a separate branch of production, hiring Roy L. McCardell as their first story editor.[14] Born in 1870 in Hagerstown, Maryland, Roy Larcom McCardell pursued a long career as a journalist, with the Birmingham *Age-Herald*, the New York *Evening Sun*, *Puck*, the New York *World*, and the New York *Sunday Telegraph* (as editor). Meanwhile, he contributed poetry and prose to *Pearson's*, *Everybody's*, *Harper's*, and *Century*, and wrote novels, musical comedies, and dramas.[15]

McCardell served on the editorial staff at *Puck*, started in 1877 as the American version of the German humour magazine of the same name. His duties at *Puck* included supervising the pioneer comic strips of Frederick Burr Opper and M.M. Howarth.[16]

McCardell subsequently moved to the New York *World*, a moribund newspaper purchased in 1883 by Joseph Pulitzer, bitter rival of William Randolph Hearst, with the intention of turning it into a modern daily paper. Among the *World*'s innovations (including big headlines, sensational stories,

Fig. 1. Roy L. McCardell, story editor at Biograph. [Photo from author's collection.]

complete with a postscript praising the socialist experiment at the Barriston Silk Mills. Foster Coates, managing editor of the *World,* called the serialisation 'the most successful feature the *Evening World* has ever had', and pugilist James J. Corbett called it 'the best story I ever read'.[18]

Fellow journalist and pioneer scenarist Epes Winthrop Sargent recalled McCardell's adventures in the mid-1900s in a 1914 article in *Motion Picture World*:

> About this time Roy McCardell ... was 'writing pictures' for the *Standard.* They were not moving pictures in the sense now employed, though they were indeed moving. McCardell used to write about ten captions telling a more or less complete story. Then he and the boss would hire a lot of models – mostly girls – and go out and make pictures for the captions.[19]

The publication Sargent referred to was the *Standard,* an entertainment weekly that was started in 1889 as *Sport, Music and Drama,* becoming *Music and Drama* in 1892, then *Standard Music and Drama* in 1893, *Standard* from 1894 to 1901, then passing through five more changes of title before becoming the modern *Vanity Fair* (1913–36).[20]

During McCardell's adventures, the *Standard* was a weekly of the popular Broadway Theatre which featured copious photo illustrations, mostly of young actresses, which celebrated the contemporary image of the saucy libertine, usually in fairly erotic display. In the early 1990s, the *Standard* featured portrait and full-figure photos. By the middle of the decade, groups of photos began to appear together, often illustrating make-up or costume sequences or key scenes of current theatrical entertainments.

However, around the time that McCardell reportedly dallied at the *Standard,* a different kind of photo feature began to appear, one which at-

sports columns, and copious illustrations) one McCardell shared credit for, that was the production of the first colour-page comic supplement featuring Richard Outcault's 'Down Hogan's Alley', precursor to the legendary 'Yellow Kid'.[17]

While at the *World* McCardell wrote under a pseudonym a serialised story of the horrors of New York factory life which prompted the outpouring of a record 7000 letters from readers and the subsequent publication of the serial by the Boston *Globe,* the Pittsburgh *Times,* the Cleveland *Press,* the Buffalo *Times,* the Augusta *Herald* and other daily newspapers. The stories were published as a novel, *The Wage Slaves of New York* in 1899,

Fig. 2. One of McCardell's photo-stories from the *Standard* (5 December 1896): 'Little Willie and the Chorus Girls, Showing how a Youthful Clerk, with Three per Week and Sporty Ideas, is Received and finally Sent Home, a Wiser Young Man' [author's collection].

tempted to tell a short, complete story, aided by written captions. These photo-stories most often featured, as Sargent observed, fetching young ladies in the various acts of changing clothes, smoking cigarettes, riding bicycles, swimming at the beach, and, generally, frolicking in beautiful company. A story line, often flimsy, held the activity together, without any 'realistic' reference to costume changes or theatrical scenes. These features represent, for us, a vital synthesis of cartoon sequencing, photography and narrative conceit. Next, Sargent speculates that:

Somebody on the Biograph must have read the *Standard*, for presently McCardell was hired to go down to Thirteenth street and Broadway and write pictures for the Mutascope, then a nickel in the slot machine. They didn't think much of the projector machine in those days. It was all mutascope.[21]

However, the contact was made; McCardell naturally drifted toward the primitive 'living picture shows' and reached an agreement with Henry Marvin, general manager of Biograph, whereby McCardell would prepare story manuscripts for that studio. Marvin previously had been dependent for film stories on the 'momentary inspiration of directors, cameramen, players, or members of the office staff'.[22] McCardell was hired to provide written story 'ideas', making him, according to Sargent, 'the first man on either side of the water to be hired for no other purpose than to write pictures'.[23]

McCardell's new salary was $150 per week, a princely sum compared to the $25 the average newspaper man was then earning. Historian Benjamin Hampton suggests that news of McCardell's salary spread quickly among reporters, who 'buzzed about the headquarters of filmmakers like flies around sugar barrels, and scenario writing soon became an occupation as definite as reporting'. Within a year, McCardell had left Biograph, but he continued writing scenarios and selling material on a freelance basis to virtually every major producer.[24]

In 1900, McCardell published a book of light verse, *Olde Love and Lavender & Other Verses*, including many poems already published in *Puck*. The volume was dedicated to H.N. Marvin of the Biograph.[25]

Two novels soon appeared, *Conversations of a Chorus Girl* in 1903 and *The Show Girl and Her Friends* in 1904, the latter illustrated in magazine style by Gene Carr, author of *Lady Bountiful*. Both were spicy evocations of nighttime Broadway theatre life, and the *dramatis personae* of *The Show Girl and Her Friends* included Lulu Lorimer, Louie Zinsheimer, Dopey McKnight, Abie Wogglebaum, Mama de Bronscombe, Harry Trimmers, Trixie McGinnis and Mr Burlap, a loveable cast of operators in nefarious operations that previewed the world of Damon Runyon. These were followed by *The Sky Scraper*, a work seemingly lost to us, and, in 1907, *Jimmy Jones: The Autobiography of an Office Boy*, the fictive memoirs of a lovable pug in a world of nubile secretaries.[26]

In 1909, a three-act comedy by McCardell, *The Gay Life*, evidently a broadly humorous account of New York's theatrical 'Bohemia', was produced on the Broadway stage, and the review of the play in the New York *Times* mentions McCardell's periodic productions of 'newspaper sketches' of similar bohemian high jinks.[27]

More importantly, during this period McCardell was a prolific scenarist. According to contemporary screenwriter Russell E. Smith (himself a veteran journalist who followed McCardell from the *World* into motion pictures, writing the scenario for *The Escape*, directed by D.W. Griffith in 1914, and co-founding the Photoplay Authors' League in the same year), by 1915 McCardell had written over *1000* produced films. Copyright records show 39 films written by McCardell registered just from 1913 to 1916, plus an additional sixteen episodes of the serial, *The Diamond From The Sky* in the same period. Hampton reports that when Fox first embarked on feature production with an adaptation of Porter Emerson Browne's play *A Fool There Was* (itself based on a popular Kipling poem), the 1915 film which launched Theda Bara's career, McCardell was chosen to write the screenplay, a fact not reflected in the film's copyright entry. Thus we can only guess at the actual extent of McCardell's screenwriting activities. In 1917, Louella O. Parsons, herself a former journalist at the Chicago *Tribune*, successful scenarist, story editor at Essanay and later premier Hollywood gossip columnist, would consider McCardell 'one of the best-known photoplaywrights in the business'.[28]

In 1916, McCardell's 'novelised' version of the infamous *The Diamond From the Sky*, the early film serial based on his prize-winning scenario, was published. Near the end of his career he published two volumes, *My Aunt Angie* (1930) and *My Uncle Oswald* (1931), in a projected four-volume anthology of the Crutch family. McCardell had been fond of comic family sagas, having written 'theatricals' about Mr and Mrs Hagg and a syndicated feature for the *World* on the continuing saga of the Jarr family, the latter giving rise to a number of produced scenarios for Vitagraph.[29]

Fig. 3. A. McCardell photo-story for *The Weekly Standard* (6 March 1897)

McCardell was clearly a prolific screenwriter who emerged from and maintained contact with many forms of popular media. He brought to film concrete experience in the creation of comic strips, popular Broadway musicals and comedies, newspaper vignettes and serials, poetry, narrative photography, and popular fiction, not to mention an awareness of the vicissitudes of writing in an institutional context like the daily newspaper. In all this he is not only early, but also exemplary of the pioneer scenarist who has a composite of skills and interests related to popular culture.

The emergence of narrative

As mentioned, the first few years of the century saw the arrival of simple story films. At the head of this rise of narrative were the films of Georges Méliès and Edwin S. Porter.

Méliès' contributions to the rise of narrative film are universally seen as vital, and historian Lewis Jacobs outlines these contributions as: the filmic creation of fantasy; the introduction of theatrical elements; the use of literature as subject matter; and, according to Jacobs :

> He also brought to movie making, with his system of 'artificially arranged scenes' [Méliès' own description of his method], a conception of organization which was to change the haphazard, improvisational methods of the Americans and fertilize their technique.[30]

This pre-production design was central to Méliès' achievements and in large part defined Méliès' work as 'scripted'. Indeed, Méliès' 'Star' catalogues contain descriptions of his films in scenario form which Jacobs regards as reproductions of the original pre-production scripts written by Méliès himself.

The scenario for the 400 foot *Cinderella*, reproduced in the 'Star' 1900–01 catalogue is little more than a listing of brief phrases describing the twenty scenes or 'motion tableaux' that make up the film. Even so, the numbering of separate scenes is significant because it reflects an awareness of the serial presentation of discrete actions segmented by

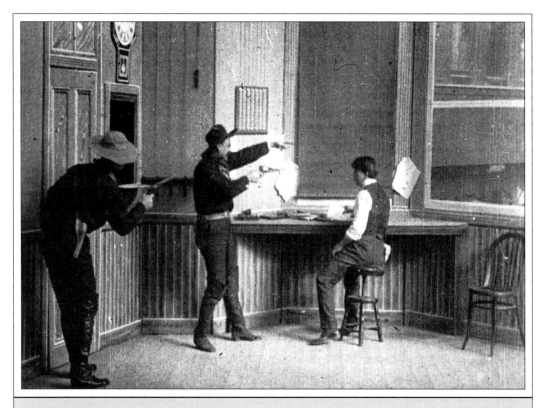

Fig. 4. Edwin S. Porter drew on pre-existing sources in constructing his scenario for *The Great Train Robbery* (Edison, 1903). [Museum of Modern Art/Film Stills Archive.]

units of production as in the basic scenario format. As Jacobs notes, this ordering of units 'did form a coherent, logical, progressive continuity' through which the filmmaker 'could control both the material and its arrangement'.[31]

The scenario for Melies' classic, the 825-foot *A Trip to the Moon*, reproduced in his 1904 catalogue, is even more intriguing. Not only are the individual activities within the scenes more detailed, but the scenario indicates a movement away from a rigid sense of the complete 'tableau' as the basic unit, as in the following sequences:

7. The monster gun. March past the gunners. Fire!!! Saluting the flag.
8. The flight through space. Approaching the moon.
9. Landed right in the eye!!!
10. Flight of the shell into the Moon. Appearance of the earth from the moon.

And:

21. The astronomers find the shell again. Departure from the moon.
22. Vertical drop into space.
23. Splashing into the open sea.
24. At the bottom of the ocean.[32]

These 'scenes' display an awareness of the ability to prescribe units shorter than a complete dramatic action, here governed by rapid change in location generated by subject movement. Such abbreviated segmentation of continuous activity would prove one of film's most fertile lines of development.

Closer to home, the Edison catalogues of 1903 and 1904 contain descriptions of Edwin S. Porter's seminal films *The Life of an American Fireman* (1903) and *The Great Train Robbery* (1903), also in scenario form.

The scenario for *The Life of an American Fireman* is particularly interesting. As Jacobs notes, not only are the individual scenes much more extensive and detailed in their description of the film's dramatic actions than Méliès in scenarios, but details of location, camera position, and filmic transition are specified. Further, the scenario prescribes specific shots, with transitions, within scenes, and one infamous scene is comprised of a single close-up – further evidence of the development of segmentation by design.[33] *The Life of an American Fireman* began, in 1902, with pre-existant film footage of a fire department in action. Greatly impressed by the length, arrangement, and segmentation of Méliès' films,[34] Porter then:

> ... planned another motion picture project. He began by writing a story in seven scenes to enable him to use [the] previously photographed film which he supplemented by shooting several new scenes to add to its excitement.[35]

The processes of preconceiving the second project and shooting the new footage resulted in a narrative structure, with parallel story developments resolving in a fortuitous rescue, a staple design for much ensuing film fare. The vital additional footage would have been virtually impossible to shoot without some prior sense of the entire story, as embodied in Porter's written plan of seven scenes. Porter's own remembrance of the procedure is telling:

> ... I often wondered why it was not possible to produce a dramatic story in motion pictures. At this period I was chief producer of the Edison Company and it seemed peculiarly proper to me for the Edison Company to inaugurate this innovation. Accordingly, *I conceived and prepared a story* called 'The Life of an American Fireman', a complete 800-foot story based on a fairly good dramatic element and introducing the fireman's life in the engine house and in his home ... Encouraged by the success of this experiment, we devoted all our resources to the production of *stories*, instead of disconnected and unrelated scenes[36] [first emphasis added].

As Porter suggested, a similar germination preceded his next film, *The Great Train Robbery*. Porter had already made a short-subject film of 'Phoebe Snow', a mythical girl dressed all in white who rode unsoiled on the Lackawana Railroad, a testament to the hygiene of rail travel. Some time later, Porter was discussing other production matters with a scene painter, who happened to mention the title of a prior stage production, *The Great Robbery*. Presumably the experience of filming on the railroad plus the mention of this pregnant title fused in Porter's mind, and, according to Ramsaye, he 'went to work on the idea, writing the memorandum of the scenes of a simple story of a train hold-up, a pursuit, a dance–hall episode, and an escape'.[37] Historian D.J. Wenden claims the film was adapted from the 1896 stage play of the same name by Scott Marple, which would make the activity of scripting both more definite and more complex, in that the basic problem of translating dialogue into activity would have to be addressed. Charles Musser suggests that the film also had sources in Wild West Shows, such as Buffalo Bill's 'Hold Up of the Deadwood Stage', and in accounts of train robberies in newspapers.[38] In either case, we have a process of a written preconception giving rise to the rehearsal of actors, and again to a story form full of related parallel developments, which would be both enormously popular with the public and hailed by later commentators as fundamental to film narrative.[39] Further, in his time at Edison, Porter 'wrote many scenarios',[40] and his own summary of this evolutionary phase is well worth noting:

> [E]ven at an early date in the history of the industry it was commonly recognised that the introduction of general dramatic principles in the production of motion pictures was desirable and necessary. The problem, however, remained as to the best means of utilising the science of drama so as to conform with the mechanical limitations of the film, and later, with the vast possibilities that these same mechanical factors presented.[41]

Porter's contributions to 'the introduction of general dramatic principles', 'utilising the science of drama', are normally reduced to the practice of editing but, as is hopefully clear, these contributions involve a much more extensive sense of design and arrangement of narrative in all phases of production. 'Editing' alone understates both Porter's achievements and the functions of both screenwrit-

Fig. 5. Gene Gauntier, writer, director and star of the early cinema, in a picture postcard view. [Richard Koszarski collection.]

was. Then we acted and photographed it, the one who was not acting turning the handle. Then we developed and printed it, and took it to our fairground customers … After that we reassembled and put our heads together *to think of another story.*[44] [emphasis added]

Beyond the appearance of these seminal films, the first decade of the century saw the narrative mode come to dominate motion pictures. Research indicates that the various forms of narrative comprised about twelve per cent of films copyrighted in 1900.[45] By 1903, comic films alone comprised 30 per cent of those copyrighted. Even as late as 1906, there were more actuality films than fiction films; but by 1908, narrative (comedy and drama) had risen to an astounding 96 per cent of those registered.[46]

It would seem difficult to overstate the importance of this arrival of narrative film. For Ramsaye it came at the lowest ebb of early motion picture popularity, (the vaudeville houses where movies were then exhibited were about to abandon them) and rescued both the medium and the industry.[47] Hampton regards the story film's superlative success as both the fulfillment of film's original

ing and directing in designing and manipulating narrative film.[42]

Another film that is often cited as a primitive exemplar of filmic narrative form, in this case plot development through the matching of temporally continuous subject actions through varied backgrounds, is Cecil Hepworth's 1905 work *Rescued by Rover*, which evolved from a scenario by Mrs Hepworth, who also acted in the film, along with the Hepworth baby and dog.[43] Hepworth's own recollection of his early production procedures is, again, telling:

> *First we thought of a story*; then we painted the scenery if it wasn't all open air, as it usually

creative promise and the impetus for the next phase of exhibition, the nickelodeon theatre:

> To the hundreds of thousands who had become screen enthusiasts in the years of episodes and storyettes, the storytelling motion pictures added millions. In every city and large town in the country so many customers appeared at ticket windows that there were not enough halls or upstairs rooms to seat them, and a new type of playhouse [the nickelodeon] had to be created to accommodate the newcomers.[48]

For Jacobs, the narrative film fuelled the very permanence of the motion picture industry:

The remarkable success of story films – The *Great Train Robbery* in particular – caused a fresh outpouring of capital into the motion picture trade. Between 1903 and 1908 the movies ascended from the level of petty commerce to that of a large, permanent business, with three distinct phases which were eventually to grow into big separate industries.[49]

Historian Robert C. Allen has suggested that the narrative film, rather than arriving as a lucky or inevitable aesthetic development, resulted from the industry's phenomenally increased demand for new films, which itself resulted from the proliferation of nickelodeons. For Allen, the narrative film satisfied the film industry's needs of meeting the increasing demand for films while gaining both a measure of control over the costs and logistics of production, and another measure of industrial stability through regularisation of production.[50] The procedures of pre-production in general and the document of the scenario in particular would necessarily be the devices for effecting such gains.

Pioneer screenwriting

Whatever the actual configuration of factors, there is little doubt that around 1905 the 800- to 1000-foot, or one-reel, narrative film emerged, along with a room of its own, the nickelodeon theatre. With the ascendancy of narrative came a rapidly rising demand for story materials to be filmed, and producers increasingly turned to the adaptation of theatre and literature for material. The triumvirate of early Chicago producers, Colonel Selig, George K. Spoor and George Kleine, even considered pooling $100,000 to corner the world market on film story rights. When his cohorts backed out, Selig himself ventured into the book market and bought up a large number of film rights at a time when their value was uncertain, including works by Mary Roberts Rinehart, Zane Gray and Winston Churchill, at prices ranging from $25 to $100. The Selig company thus acquired a considerable library of novels and plays at bargain prices, and many of these rights would become extremely valuable by the mid-1910s.[51]

Purchased or not, such use of theatrical and literary materials obviously necessitated routine adaptation, and early screenwriters increasingly functioned to transform story material into scenarios, which were often simply lists of the scenes to be shot, in the order of their eventual appearance in the edited film, close to our modern master-scene format, and not unlike the earlier Méliès or Edison catalogue descriptions. Even an aspiring D.W. Griffith first visited the Edison studio in 1907 with a scenario 'adapted' from *La Tosca* in hand.[52]

Also in 1907, playwright and journalist Stanner E.V. Taylor was hired as a staff scenarist by Biograph. Taylor, disconsolate over the sudden closing of his musical comedy *The Gibson Girl*, was recruited in an empty New York restaurant late one night by Arthur Marvin, who was scouting directing and writing talent for the then lowly Biograph. Taylor signed on for a $25 a week guarantee, married Biograph actress Marion Leonard and remained an active screenwriter for over two decades for Biograph, Reliance, Monopole, Mutual and other producers. There is no telling just how many scenarios Taylor wrote during his prolific career because a good portion of his output at Biograph went unrecorded. His known story and writing credits include: *The Adventures of Dollie* (1908); *Leather Stockings* (1909); *Lines of White on a Sullen Sea* (1909); *A Child of the Ghetto* (1910); *In the Border States* (1910); *A Midnight Cupid* (1910); *What the Daisy Said* (1910); *Her Father's Pride* (1910); *The Squaw's Love* (1911); *In the North Woods* (1912); *Day's Outing* (1913); *Yaqui Cur* (1913); *Leaf in the Storm* (1913); *The Seed of the Fathers* (1913); *The Light Unseen* (1914); *Mother Love* (1914); *Passers By* (1916); *Her Great Hour* (1916); *The Public Be Damned* (1917); *The Hun Within* (1918); *The Great Love* [1918]; *The Greatest Thing in Life* [1919] and *A Romance of Happy Valley* [1919] were written in collaboration with D.W. Griffith under the pseudonym Capt. Victor Maurier); *The Girl Who Stayed at Home* (1919); *Scarlet Days* (1919); *Boots* (1919); *The Idol Dancer* (1920); *Nothing But Lies* (1920); *The Very Idea* (1920); *The Mohican's Daughter* (1922); *The Lone Wolf* (1924); *The Miracle of Life* (1926); *King Cowboy* (1928); *Breed of the Sunsets* (1928); *Dog Law* (1928) and *The Red Sword* (1929).[53]

Again in 1907, Miss Gene Gauntier, perhaps the first woman staff scenarist and later a leading actress, director and eventually an independent producer, prepared a 'working synopsis' for the Kalem Company's spectacular one-reel production of *Ben Hur*, an effort notable on two counts.[54]

First, besides the significant role of translating written literary material into a plan of activity, the brevity of such a film would have demanded much selection and arrangement in condensing the original material into one reel, an additional aspect of much of the early adaptation for silent film.

Second, Kalem failed to acquire any rights to the film *Ben Hur* because the necessity of such rights was not yet firmly established and the practice of unauthorised use of extant material was widespread. But Kalem was subsequently sued by Harper & Brothers, publishers of the novel; Klaw and Erlanger, producers of the stage version; and the estate of the deceased author, Lew Wallace. The case ascended to the Supreme Court, which in 1911 ruled against Kalem, prescribing a $25,000 royalty payment and establishing the application of copyrights to films' use of story material. The dramatic structure of film was thus regarded as a tangible property (the term would stick and become a near-perfect metonymy in production parlance) of legal stature and commercial value, two rather telling measures which would have profound effects on screenwriting.[55]

However, in 1908 the Supreme Court ruling was yet to come, and there were other, more immediate changes in the film industry affecting screenwriting.

Nickelodeon theatres multiplied rapidly, and by 1910 there were 10,000 of them across the country. This phenomenal growth in exhibition outlets from 1905 to 1910 generated a massive demand for films, which in turn necessitated large-scale production by the then barely organised manufacturers. The result was the evolution of a new level of production organisation. Large, well-equipped, indoor studios were constructed which utilised interior lighting and were capable of housing much more regular, reliable operations than were possible with location shooting or natural light studios. Such expanded, regularised production required not only more filmmaking personnel, but the efficiency of specialisation or division of labour. In an art form already complex, even collaborative, such individual crafts as directing, acting, cinema-

tography, and laboratory work became increasingly distinct and developed.[56]

Obviously, the pre-production design of narrative films fit well into this evolving studio system, as written design was by its very written nature procedurally distinct from other aspects of production. Thus, in addition to the intrinsic factors of the narrative mode itself and the increasing length of films, the extrinsic factors of large-scale production and the evolving studio system surely helped institutionalise screenwriting. The evolving studio system advanced not only the craft of screenwriting, but also the separate role of the scenario or story editor, who managed the various aspects of the studio's use of story materials and writing skills. Clifford Howard, an early screenwriter and scenario editor, later recalled this evolution:

> Out of the early scenario writers came the scenario editor. As the movie industry developed there arose the need for someone to relieve the director of the task which originally fell to his lot of handling the scripts submitted to the studio, selecting the picture material, and editing such of the scenarios as were chosen for filming. Directing a picture was found to be enough of a job in itself; and so the scenario editor was called into being. And with this advent came the germ of the scenario department, destined to become one of the most important and most expensive features of a studio.[57]

Howard, a native of Pennsylvania with a law degree from Columbia University and a literary background including published novels and magazine articles, began his film career in 1908 by mail from Los Angeles, selling a twenty-scene scenario for the split-reel (500-foot) comedy *The Woman in the Case* to Vitagraph for ten dollars, and soon followed with a sale of a 45-scene, one-reel 'feature' to Biograph. After much screenwriting he became scenario editor for Balboa in 1913 and American in 1915.[58]

By 1911, *Moving Picture World* could report that the operations of the average scenario department were highly organised and that the typical scenario editor was passing judgement on 60 scenarios a day.[59]

In addition to Howard and Lee Dougherty at

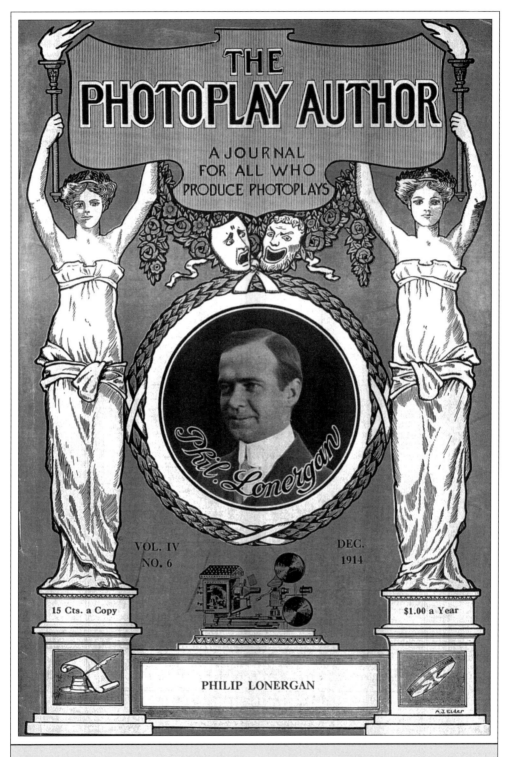

Fig. 6. Phil Lonergan on the cover of *The Photoplay Author* (IV, 6) (December 1914). [Richard Koszarski collection.]

Biograph, other early scenario editors included: Sam Pedon, Rollin S. Sturgeon, Marguerite Bertsch, Beta Breuil, and Colonel Jasper E. Brady at Vitagraph; Epes Winthrop Sargent and Lawrence McClosky at Lubin; H. Tipton Steck, Archer McMackin and Edward T. Lowe, Jr., at Essanay; Phil Lang at Kalem; Edwin S. Porter and Ashley Miller at Edison; Benjamin P. Schulberg and Harry Durant at Famous Players; Richard Willis, Willis Robards, Charles M. Seay, and Herbert Brenon at IMP; Calder Johnstone, Monte Katterjohn, James Dayton, and Captain Leslie T. Peacocke at Universal; Richard V. Spencer at New York Motion Picture Company; Howell Hansel at Solax; Frank Woods at Fine Arts; Catherine Carr at North American; Hettie Gray Baker at Bosworth; Eustace Hale Ball at Reliance, Eclair, Solax, and Majestic; C.B. 'Pop' Hoadley at IMP, Champion, Great Northern and Powers; and June Mathis, who would become a super-star scenarist and production manager in the early 1920s at Metro.

In 1908, the Motion Picture Patents Company formed its infamous trust between major producers of films and equipment in the interests of ending litigation among themselves and dominating the industry. The ensuing years would be marked by a struggle between the Trust and an emerging group of independent producers for industry control, and, as we shall see, this struggle would have great effects on screenwriting.

Among the independents that emerged was the Thanhouser Corporation, notable for its initial attitude toward screenwriting and its nurturing of a prolific scenarist, Lloyd Lonergan.

Lonergan was a graduate of the Annapolis Naval Academy, a successful magazine writer and a veteran journalist at the New York *World* when in 1909 his brother-in-law Edwin Thanhouser, started a film production company in New Rochelle, New York. Lonergan was lured to New Rochelle, and observed that film industry sources advised his brother-in-law to hire good directors and let the directors worry about the stories. Lonergan recalled:

> But the man who is now my boss couldn't see it that way. He had had a long experience in the theatrical game, made a name for himself with his stock company in Milwaukee, and

persisted in the belief that the pictures were a form of dramatic art.

'When I had my theatrical company', he said, 'I never told the director, "Go and put on a play", and trusted to his inventive genius. I selected a manuscript I liked, and he followed it. And I didn't see any reason why the same course shouldn't be a success in the motion picture game'.[60]

Lonergan went on to write a major portion of Thanhouser's output, some 900 produced scenarios by 1915, and to become head of production. With the addition of brother Phillip, a scenarist for Thanhouser and Majestic, and sister Elizabeth, a veteran magazine writer for *Strand* and scenarist for Biograph, Kalem and Majestic, the Lonergans formed an early screenwriting family, alongside the Hoadleys, 'Pop' and Harold.[61]

If the development of the studio system further distinguished the craft of screenwriting, the growth of censorship provided an additional vantage on the evolving role of the scenario in production. Responding to local efforts to control the content of the movies, the National Board of Censorship of Motion Pictures was formed in 1909 for the purpose of reviewing films and providing a seal of approval for those without offense.[62] Subsequent instruction in screenwriting would describe forbidden elements at length and emphasise that no producer should be expected to purchase material containing such elements. One writing manual suggested:

> Inasmuch as the National Board, from a trade standpoint, is almost entirely in the nature of an insurance for the manufacturers that valuable reels will not be thrown back on their hands *after* the printing and distribution through the country ... it behooves the scenario writer to insure their financial return and ... reputation ... by a thorough understanding of and even sympathy with the fundamentals from which the Board's critique is carried on.[63]

Clearly, if filmmakers were to effect some degree of self-censorship, the scenario was the critical phase of production at which to exercise prior restraint. Such policy, however lamentable, demonstrates once again the screenplay's ability to embody vital features for the ensuing film.

Of all the early scenarists, Frank E. 'Spec' Woods would become the dean, a position that was acknowledged when his colleagues chose him as the first president of the Photoplay Authors' League in 1914.

Born in Linesville, Pennsylvania, Frank Emerson Woods began his long career in journalism editing his high school paper, and by age eighteen was publishing his own daily in Erie, Pennsylvania. Woods then gravitated toward theatrical printing, having his own firm in Massillon, Ohio, in the 1890s, then moved on to New York.[64]

In 1907 Woods, by then a veteran newsman, was a reporter and advertising solicitor for the New York *Dramatic Mirror*. At this time a feud broke out between the eminent stage actress Minnie Maddern Fiske, a major stockholder in the *Mirror*, and her theatrical producers, Klaw and Erlanger, who heatedly withdrew their substantial advertising business from Mrs Fiske's paper. Woods was then sent to seek advertising from the vulgar realms of the motion picture industry, previously disregarded by the *Mirror* and other theatrical publications. As an incentive for this new clientele, Woods was given regular space in the *Mirror*, titled the 'Moving Picture Department', to cover the movies, and in 1908 Woods inaugurated regular newspaper reviewing of films under the byline 'The Spectator'. These reviews were surprisingly critical, erudite, and not without salutary effects on film producers. As a result of this coverage of motion pictures, the *Dramatic Mirror* prospered; the film industry received serious trade press consideration, and Woods became chief editor.[65]

Through his film industry contacts Woods became acquainted with Lee Dougherty, Biograph's advertising manager and first scenario editor. Woods soon began to sell story 'suggestions' to Dougherty, and among these suggestions was Biograph's first detailed continuity script, a version of Tennyson's poem *Enoch Arden*, which was produced under D.W. Griffith's direction for the first of

Fig. 7. Frank E. Woods, c. 1915. [Richard Koszarski collection.]

two times as *After Many Years* in 1908. At the same time, Woods sold the story for the first of the series of 'Jones' farces, which Griffith also directed in 1909.[66]

In 1912, Woods moved to California where he wrote and directed for Kinemacolor. Within a year that company folded and Woods joined Universal for six unhappy weeks as a staff writer. He then returned to New York, Biograph, and his close association with Griffith, working on the titles for *Judith of Bethulia* (1913).[67] Moving to Mutual with Griffith, Woods brought to Griffith's attention a property, produced but unreleased at Kinemacolor, for which Woods had written the continuity, Thomas Dixon's play *The Clansman*. Woods shared the screenwriting credit with Griffith for the ensuing film, *The Birth of a Nation* (1915).[68] After substantial collaboration with Griffith, Woods gravitated toward the business end of filmmaking and was later associated with Thomas Ince, Mack Sennett, Famous Players–Lasky, and Paramount. Epes Winthrop Sargent credits Woods with being 'the one commentator on the photoplay who never wrote a book on how to do it'.[69]

Like the work of Stanner E.V. Taylor, much of Woods' screenwriting at Biograph went unrecorded. His known writing credits include: *After Many Years* (1908); *Mr Jones at the Ball*, etc. (1908+); *The Marked Timetable* (1910); *Mugsy's First Sweetheart* (1910); *Simple Charity* (1910); *Mr Grouch at the Seashore* (1912); *At the Basket Picnic* (1912); *The Reformer* (1913); *Left-Handed Man* (1913); *In Diplomatic Circles* (1913); *The Mirror* (1913); *The Stopped Clock* (1913); *Judith of Bethulia* (1913); *The Mountain Rat* (1914); *The Absentee* (1915); *The Birth of a Nation* (1915); *A Man's Prerogative* (1915); *The Children Pay* (1916); *The Little School Ma'am* (1916); *The Bad Boy* (1917); *Betsy's Burglar* (1917); *An Old Fashioned Young Man* (1917); *A Woman's Awakening (1917); A Prince There Was* (1921); *The Old Homestead* (1922); *Richard the Lion-Hearted* (1923); *Loving Lies* (1924); *What Shall I Do?* (1924) and *Let Women Alone* (1925).

When, back in 1908, Woods sold his first batch of 'suggestions' to Biograph, he returned to the *Dramatic Mirror* and spread his gain, nine five-dollar bills, across an office table. Among the dazzled newsmen present was George W. Terwilliger, who quickly followed Woods to Biograph, where he sold a scenario entitled *The Guerrilla*, based on an unproduced vaudeville playlet that Terwilliger had written which called for a mixture of live stage action and projected motion picture footage. It was filmed by Biograph, under Griffith's direction, in 1908, the first of Griffith's many Civil War stories.

Terwilliger continued writing scenarios for Biograph and moved to the New York *Telegraph*, where he established a motion picture department under the byline 'George Trent'. Terwilliger then moved on to staff screenwriting positions with Reliance and Lubin, where he became a director.[70]

In 1910 another notable figure, Emmett Campbell Hall, entered the field of screenwriting. Born in 1882 in Tolbottom, Georgia, Hall went north to Washington, DC, for schooling, graduated from the National Law School, and entered the diplo-

matic bureau of the State Department. After some publication of short stories and verse in magazines, Hall sold his first scenario in 1910 to the Lubin company, titled *Indian Blood*, reputedly the first of the 'reversion to type' or genetically tragic film stories. Hall insisted on remaining home in Glen Echo, Maryland, and working freelance. His specialty was the Civil War period, and he sold Biograph scenarios for *The House with the Closed Shutters* (1910), *His Trust* (1911) and *His Trust Fulfilled* (1911), all directed by Griffith. By July 1911, Hall figured he had sold about 90 per cent of the scenarios he had written in the open market, a total of somewhere over 100 screenplays. In 1913, Hall was coaxed into joining the Lubin scenario staff, but soon fled the big city for his Maryland home. He continued to write freelance, and by 1923 had over 700 original scenarios produced by fifteen studios, plus numerous adaptations.[71]

Another former newsman who broke into screenwriting with Biograph was William E. Wing, a native of Maine and graduate of the University of Southern California who had been a reporter on the Minneapolis *Tribune* and in 1897 returned to Los Angeles to become the local correspondent for the *Dramatic Mirror*. When Biograph moved west in 1911, Wing became acquainted with scenario editor Lee Dougherty. Wing later recalled:

> Dougherty proved to be my real downfall. He listened to my jokesome remarks anent movie stories, and turned the tables on me inside of ten minutes. He asked me what I would call a good plot for a photoplay. I told him one. He proceeded to prove that it was not a plot, not even a plot's little brother. This so chagrined me I fought back with other plots. Mr Dougherty, the first editor of any studio, kindly forgave me and lent me aid. In time I was writing for the Biograph.[72]

Wing wrote over 80 produced scenarios from 1913 to 1917 for Biograph, Selig, Fine Arts, Vitagraph, and National, including *By Man's Law* (directed by Griffith, 1913), the *Tomboy Bessie* (1913) comedy series featuring Mabel Normand, *Hope* (1913), *The Heart of Maggie Malone* (1914), *Sold For Marriage* (1916), *Little Miss Adventure* (1916), *The Hat* (1916) and *Tarzan of the Apes* (1917). He and his wife, Maria A. Wing, formed an early husband/wife writing team, alongside contemporaries Frank and Nancy Ellen Anderson Woods, Anne and Bannister Merwin, and Anita Loos and John Emerson. By 1923, 400 of Wing's original scenarios had been produced.[73]

At Biograph, Griffith encouraged not only the careers of the newsmen/scenarists, but also the contribution of original story material from within his stock company, offering fifteen dollars for story 'ideas'. Mary Pickford contributed scenarios in this manner (*Madam Rex*, 1911; *Lena and the Geese*, 1912), as did Mack Sennett (*Trying to Get Arrested*, 1909; *The Lonedale Operator*, 1911), who early on favoured tales featuring comic policemen.[74]

There is no avoiding the question of Griffith's relationship to screenwriting. It has become a truism of history that Griffith never used a script which, if it means that he did not use one on the set, seems to have some solid corroboration, including the memoirs of actress Lillian Gish and cameraman Karl Brown. This reported practice is often taken to mean that Griffith's films did not pass through some phase of written de-

Fig. 8. Anita Loos, one of Douglas Fairbanks' screenwriters. [Courtesy of John Belton.]

sign, and are cinematically 'purer' for having avoided verbal corruption. It is, however, appropriate to consider Griffith's early work as a playwright and scenarist, including his scenarios for *Old Isaacs, the Pawnbroker, The Music Master, At the Crossroads of Life, The Stage Rustler* and *Ostler Joe*.[75]

Regarding the possible absence of screenwriting from the Griffith-production enterprise, feature film historian Kenneth Macgowan noted in 1919:

Film editing, directing and continuity writing are [Griffith's] regular tasks, as those who have

read of his making of 'The Birth of a Nation' know. But it is further true that Griffith is frequently the creator of the idea, the builder of the synopsis. There was once a certain 'Granville Warwick', unknown to studio directors but prominent on the credit titles of many Triangle productions ... When David Wark Griffith dropped out of Triangle, 'Warwick' dropped with him. And until Griffith came back from Europe, 'Warwick' was silent ... Perhaps he is a relative of the mysterious Monsieur Gaston de Tolignac, who has been 'suggesting' or 'conceiving' other European-born Griffith products. But, however that may be, nobody who knows the Griffith studio denies that D.G. is as skillful a scenario writer as he is a director.[76]

Griffith would subsequently add the names of Roy Sinclair and Irene Sinclair to his roster of fictitious scenarists. In 1915, pioneer scenarist Russell E. Smith, who in 1915 regarded Griffith as 'the most expert script writer of the business'.[77] The actual range of Griffith's skills was suggested by scenarist Jeanie Macpherson in a 1922 article, in which she was emphasising the extreme dangers to film's dramatic structure of unbalanced directorial power:

> Strange as it may seem, some of the biggest and best pictures have been produced by this method, but that was simply because it happened that the director in each case was an artist and a screen dramatist as well as an actor–director.[78]

The star system, feature films, and the copyright law

In 1910, a front-page article in the trade publication *Moving Picture World* raised the question of regular screen credits for scenarists. Noting that in the preceding year the public had become 'unmistakably interested in the personalities of the chief performers' and that Edison, Selig, and other producers were advertising the names of famous authors of those story properties they were adapting to the screen, the article asked its readers to send in their opinions on whether scenarists should be given screen credits and thus be allowed to develop a public following.[79]

The article suggests that while scenarists would gain much stature 'inside' the industry and, curiously, the craft itself would soon gain great publicity 'outside', the individual scenarist would never acquire that public distinction the article proposed. This complex obscurity would hang over the screenwriter indefinitely.

However, in noting the issue of screen credits and the rising public interest in 'chief performers', the article touched on factors which would fundamentally alter the industry. As noted, the formation of the Motion Picture Patents Company's Trust in 1908 initiated a struggle between the Trust and independent producers for control of the industry.

The major innovations that accompanied this struggle were the public identification of players and the continuing evolution in film length, both seemingly thwarted by Trust policies. The former would result in the star system and the latter in the feature film. Both would have great bearing on screenwriting.[80]

The star system forced scenarists to address those aspects of character in film narrative which were generated by the personality of the player.[81] Thus, certain key scenarists became intimately involved in the creation or sustenance of clearly defined screen personas for particular stars, such as Anita Loos for Douglas Fairbanks, Frances Marion for Mary Pickford and C. Gardner Sullivan for William S. Hart. The star system required screenplays, in addition to all their other functions, to serve as precise 'vehicles' for pre-established screen personalities in characteristic narrative patterns. Further, while the players were certainly the true stars, some screenwriters, such as McCardell, Sullivan, and Hampton Del Ruth, would profit handsomely from the general ascendancy of talent that marked the later 1910s, becoming financial, if not visible, stars themselves.

In addition, the evolution of film length past the Trust's one-reel standard clearly affected screenwriters. Arbitrary limits on length were viewed by scenarists as unnatural and detrimental to storytelling. In 1911, films up to five reels in length began arriving from Europe. In October of 1911, W. Stephen Bush reported in *Moving Picture World* that:

> Within the last six months the production of subjects, consisting of two or more reels, has shown a marked increase. The most notable of them, Dante's 'Inferno' and Torquato Tasso's 'Jerusalem Delivered', the former in five and the latter in four reels, have been produced in Europe and marketed in this country independently of any organisation of filmmakers. The success of these two features has greatly stimulated a trend toward releases of greater length among American manufacturers, who had begun to give the possibilities of longer films their earnest attention. As a result releases of greater length have become numerous in both Licensed [Trust] and Independent camps.

There is every reason to believe that this tendency toward feature films of greater length will continue ...[82]

Also in 1911, Griffith's two-reel *Enoch Arden* was released and, like the European imports, exhibited a reel at a time until audience demand prompted showing both reels together.[83] By February 1912, Epes Winthrop Sargent would report that 'almost overnight the two-, three- and five-reel subject has come into its own'.[84]

The arrival of the feature film was another milestone for the screenwriter. Since pre-production, design was a natural concomitant of the narrative mode itself; increasing film length and complexity of production led to greater reliance upon the screenplay as a blueprint for production.

Alongside the star system and the feature film came the 1911 Supreme Court ruling restricting the use of theatrical and literary source materials. Producers were obliged to honor copyright laws and pay for the use of material not in the public domain, and the already intense demand for original stories exploded. Producers began aggressively soliciting the submission of original material, from known writers, the photoplay agencies and brokers that were springing up, and the general public.

The active encouragement of public submission of original story material was not an entirely new practice. As early as 1897, the American Mutoscope Company had advertised a five-dollar payment for 'suggestions for a good scene', preferably comic, on their Mutoscope bulletins. In 1909, Vitagraph had started distributing instruction sheets on scenario formats to the public, and about the same time Essanay began advertising for scripts in the writers' magazine *The Editor*, announcing: 'We pay from $10 to $100, no literary experience required.'

However, now the cultivation of the public was in earnest. Many producers began using the burgeoning fan and trade magazines to inform the public of this exotic new opportunity, and most gave out instructions or 'form sheets' on scenario formats.[85] Soon even *Moving Picture World* established a regular feature on scenario writing, headed by Epes Winthrop Sargent, to teach the craft to its readers.

Epes Winthrop Sargent

One could hardly descend from more illustrious lineage than Epes Winthrop Sargent VI. His ancestors William and Mary Epes Sargent emigrated from England to the Gloucester settlement of the Massachusetts Bay Company some time prior to 1678. Their son Epes, colonel of militia in the Revolutionary War, was the first in the American line of Sargents, which would produce an incredible number of statesmen, scholars, authors and artists. This bluest of Yankee clans would mingle with the lines of Winthrop, Dudley, Turner, Osborne, Coffin, Dana, Taft, Freemont, Chase, Percy, Singer and so on.

Epes VI was born 31 August 1872 in Nassau, the Bahamas, where his father, Epes Dixwell Sargent V, a medical doctor formerly in the drug business in Maine and Boston, had come to engage in the shipping trade. During the Civil War, Epes V fought Confederate blockade runners on their way to Charleston, and after the war he brought both the successful treatment of yellow fever and telephone service to Nassau, while serving as the West Indies correspondent for the Detroit *Free Press*. In 1880 the family returned to the United States, where Epes V served in the Navy Department in Washington, DC, and later moved to New York and opened a drug store.[86]

From a youth spent ushering at the Bijou Theatre in Washington, Epes VI launched a career in amusement trade journalism in 1891, first covering minor musical concerts for the New York *Musical Courier* for three years, then becoming vaudeville editor at Leander Richardson's *Dramatic News*, a theatrical journal. When that publication failed in 1896 and was taken over by the *Daily Mercury* (a horse racing and theatrical sheet) Sargent stayed on with the *Mercury*.[87]

Sargent's reigning passion was vaudeville but, according to historian Douglas Gilbert, 'at this time – the early 1890s – publishers took heed only of vaudeville acts that advertised and reserved their reviews for legit shows'.[88] Sargent dearly wanted to give vaudeville some needed critical attention, and wrote a number of caustic reviews which went unpublished. One Sunday, when there was a shortage of copy, a Sargent review was accidentally printed, unsigned, under the heading, 'Chatter of

Fig. 9. The cover of the first issue of *Variety*, with Epes Winthrop Sargent featured as 'Chicot'. [Author's collection.]

Chicot, the court jester to Henry III in Dumas' *La Dame de Monsoreau* and *Les Quarante-Cing*, is one of Dumas' most enduring characters. An all-licenced fool, yet finally wise, loyal and valuable to his king, he is regarded as Dumas' Falstaff.

Sargent's Chicot sallied forth with his fool's licence. According to Gilbert:

This column proved to be one of the most provocative departments ever printed in a newspaper, and Chicot's influence on the development of vaudeville can hardly be overestimated. Managers and public accepted his analyses at first skeptically, then with enthusiasm. Both were grateful for guidance, and lazy or indifferent performers, realising that bad notices might lead to cancellation, sought to better their routines. Chicot became an important figure on Broadway, respected and liked by some, hated, feared, and yet admired by most. But he hit hard and was generally loathed throughout the circuits. Often he was threatened with physical violence. A fighter himself, he responded in person to all letters suggesting he meet the aggrieved performer.[90]

Music Halls'. It was well received and became a regular feature. As *Daily Mercury* features normally carried a byline, Sargent was approached on this matter and the result was, as he recalled, the birth of his infamous pseudonym:

My stuff was unsigned for several months, but I kept writing in the first person and finally was told to select a name. I offered that my own name was good enough, but they had other reasons. I had just finished reading one of Dumas' works and suggested, 'Why not make it Chicot? He was as big a fool as he looked'. 'How do you spell it?' and the signature was created.[89]

Sargent/Chicot then left the *Daily Mercury* to cover vaudeville for the *Germanic News*, but in the mid-1890s moved to the New York *Morning Telegraph*, a sports and theatrical paper that had taken over the *Mercury*. Again, Chicot's caustic reviews prompted a series of altercations with managers and performers, a circumstance not entirely unusual in that day, when critics were generally considered fair game for artists when spotted out on the boulevards.

Chicot's special targets were lackluster performances and dishonest business practices. A press agent for the Keith and Albee circuit estimated that

Chicot's muckraking was costing Albee $20,000 a year.

Meanwhile, Sargent was contributing material elsewhere, writing stories for *Metropolitan* magazine and the McClure newspaper syndicate, to which he had by 1908 contributed several hundred stories over various signatures, including Colin S. Colins, Lulu Johnson, Taylor White, T.S. Boyd, and William F. Bryan, most of them published by the Boston *Globe*.

In 1903, Sargent left the *Morning Telegraph*, and after a brief stint at the New York *Evening World* moved on in 1905 to help Sime Silverman found *Variety* and become its associate editor. He took the infamous name Chicot with him, prompting a lawsuit which Sargent eventually won. Photos of both Sime and Chicot were prominently featured on the cover of *Variety's* first issue, although Sargent is virtually written out of *Variety's* official history. Within six months he left *Variety* to found his own version, the short-lived *Chicot's Weekly*.[91]

Given the extensive interaction between vaudeville and early motion pictures, it was only fitting that Sargent would be smitten by the movies.[92] He started selling story ideas to film producers in 1898, the first to Vitagraph. In 1906 he entered the business side of entertainment full time, and after a year as 'press representative' for the Proctor theatres and a brief time on the press staff of William Morris, then vaudeville agents, Sargent became a pioneer press agent within the motion picture industry for various producers before settling down to screenwriting.

In 1909, Sargent became the scenario editor at the Lubin company for just over a year. It was at Lubin that most of his scenarios were produced, several hundred by his own count (also two at IMP, two at Vitagraph, and seven at Edison), mostly split-reel comedies, including one written under duress in 42 minutes and, in the same spirit, eight in five days.[93]

Sargent continued writing short stories and 'novelettes', published in *New Age, Ocean, Argosy, All Story, New York Review* and *Green Book*, throughout this period of screenwriting.

It was also fitting that Sargent would bring his critical passions to his new medium. In 1909, he began writing film criticism as Chicot for the *Film Index*; in 1911 for the *Kinematograph and Lantern Weekly* (London); and for the *Moving Picture World*

when it absorbed the *Index* in 1911. From 1912 to 1918 he wrote a regular column, 'Thinks and Things', under the byline 'Gorenflot', for the *Photoplay Author* (later the *Writers Monthly*). At the *Moving Picture World* he wrote generally on the movies and specifically on scenario writing, contributing a regular column on screenwriting titled 'Technique of the Photoplay' starting in 1911, changing to 'The Scenario Writer' later that year, and finally called 'The Photoplaywright' from 1912 to 1919 (*Photoplay* soon instituted a similar department, under various titles and editors, including its managing editor Arthur Winfield Thomas and veteran scenarist Marc Edmund Jones, appearing from 1912 until 1916, and *Moving Picture News* ran a similar feature by William Lord Wright).[94] As a gauge of Sargent's catholic sensibilities, he contributed another regular column to *Moving Picture World* titled 'Advertising for the Exhibitor', a rich collection of trade information, and in 1912 *Photoplay* editor Thomas observed that 'Sargent has had more experience in photoplay work, editorial writing and criticising, than any other man of our acquaintance'.[95]

Through his extensive writing about the motion picture, Sargent is generally credited, along with Frank Woods, W. Stephen Bush, Louis Reeves Harrison and Arthur W. Thomas, with doing what Chicot had already done for vaudeville, helping to refine the art through intelligent, uncompromising criticism.[96]

In 1928, Sargent returned to *Variety* to review films. Chicot was shortened to 'Chic', in compliance with Silverman's strict policy of four-letter pseudonyms, and Chic graced *Variety's* pages until Sargent's death in 1938. Sargent's career, like McCardell's, represents a vital confluence between media of popular culture and, like Woods', an effective combination of critical and creative sensibilities.

By 1911, a network of factors promoting the pre-production design of films was operating. The fictional narrative mode itself, with its seeming affinity for design, heightened by its own growing complexity of materials and evolving length, had come to dominate motion pictures, reaching a culmination, albeit a temporary one, in the feature film.

In addition, a bundle of external factors invited written pre-production design in the form of the screenplay. The phenomenal growth of motion picture production attending the nickelodeon theatre created an enormous demand for story materials. The studio system accentuated the craft specialisation and division of labour that was natural to written design. Censorship militated for pre-production control of story materials. The star system necessitated the careful creation and nurture of narrative vehicles for pre-established characters and story patterns. The application of copyright law to film's use of story materials made such materials suddenly valuable, either as properties to be adapted or original scenarios.

A host of early screenwriters attended these early developments. With a distinct role and identity as early as 1898, they emerged from rich backgrounds throughout the popular culture, including journalism, graphic arts, theatre and literature, and contribute creative and critical sensibilities to the emerging motion picture.♠

Notes

1. Kevin Brownlow, *The Parade's Gone By* (New York: Knopf, 1968), 308.

2. David Robinson, *The History of World Cinema* (New York: Stein and Day, 1974), 71.

3. There is little or no treatment of screenwriting or screenwriters prior to their use by Ince and subsequently until the arrival of sound in general film histories. Both the craft and writers fare better in the standard works on silent film history, which supplied the background material for this discussion, including: Benjamin B. Hampton, *History of the American Film Industry from Its Beginnings to 1931* (1931; rpt. New York: Dover, 1970); Lewis Jacobs, *The Rise of the American Film: A Critical History* (1939; rpt. New York: Teachers College Press, 1968); Kenneth Macgowan, *Behind the Screen: The History and Technique of the Motion Picture* (New York: Delacorte, 1965); and Terry Ramsaye, *A Million and One Nights: A History of the Motion Picture* (New York: Simon & Schuster, 1926). Ramsaye provides the most coverage of individual pioneer scenarists; Jacobs provides the best sense of the institutional evolution of the craft. However, nowhere is there adequate treatment of: the careers and contributions of such pioneer scenarists as Roy McCardell, Frank Woods, Epes Winthrop Sargent, Jeanie Macpherson, C. Gardner Sullivan, etc.; the vital presence of the craft prior to 1912; nor its evolution and magnitude in the 1910s.

4. A standard explication of design. See, for example, David W. Pye, *The Nature of Design* (London: Studio Vista, 1964).

5. Charles Musser, *The Emergence of Cinema: The American Screen to 1907* (New York: Scribner's, 1990), 16–17.

6. Marshall Deutelbaum, 'Structural Patterning in the Lumiere Films', *Wide Angle*, 3, no. 1 (1978): 28–37.

7. 'Lumière – The Last Interview', *Sight and Sound*, 17 (Summer 1948): 68–70; reprinted in Harry M. Geduld, ed., *Film Makers on Film Making* (Bloomington: Indiana University Press, 1967), 24.

8. Kemp R. Niver, *The First Twenty Years: A Segment of Film History* (Los Angeles: Artisan Press, 1968), 60; Ramsaye, 286–288.

9. Ramsaye, 366–378.

10. A. Nicholas Vardac, *Stage to Screen: Theatrical Method from Garrick to Griffith* (Cambridge: Harvard University Press, 1949), 109.

11. Ramsaye, 370.

12. 'The Confessions of a Scenario Editor', *Photoplay* (August 1914): 166.

13. Hampton, 29–44; Joseph H. North, *The Early Development of the Motion Picture* (1887–1909) (New York: Arno Press, 1973), 193–200; Vardac, 169–173.

14. Epes Winthrop Sargent, 'The Literary Side of Pictures', *Moving Picture World*, 21 (11 July 1914): 199; Hampton, 30.

15. 'Studio Directory', *Motion Picture News* (21 October 1916), 133.

16. Russell E. Smith, 'The Authors of the Photoplay', *Book News Monthly* (March 1915), 327.

17. Pierre Couperie *et al.*, *A History of the Comic Strip*, trans. Eileen B. Hennessy (New York: Crown, 1968), 19; Smith, 327.

18. Roy L. McCardell, *The Wage Slaves of New York* (New York: G. W. Dillingham, 1899), 9–10, endnotes.

19. Epes Winthrop Sargent, 'The Literary Side of Pictures', 199.

20. Edna Brown Titus, ed., *Union List of Serials in Libraries of the United States and Canada*, 3rd edn. (New York: H.H. Wilson, 1965), vol. 5, 4353.

21. Epes Winthrop Sargent, 'The Literary Side of Pictures', 199.

22. Hampton, 30.

23. Epes Winthrop Sargent, 'The Literary Side of Pictures', 199.

24. Hampton, 30; Smith, 327.

25. Roy L. McCardell, *Olde Love and Lavender & Other Verses* (New York: Godfrey A.S. Wieners, 1900).

26. Roy L. McCardell, *Conversations of a Chorus Girl* (New York: Street & Smith, 1903); *The Show Girl and Her Friends* (New York: Street & Smith, 1904), *Jimmy Jones: The Autobiography of an Office Boy* (Boston: Dana Estes, 1907).

27. *New York Times* (20 April 1909), 9.

28. Smith, 327; Hampton, 123; Louella O. Parsons, *How To Write for the 'Movies'*, rev. edn. (Chicago: A.C. McClurg, 1917), 37. Miss Parsons' background is described in Smith, 329. She was considered among the 'top notch' scenarists of the time by Arthur W. Thomas, 'The Photoplaywrights' Department', *Photoplay* (September 1914), 162.

29. Roy L. McCardell, The Diamond from the Sky (New York: G.W. Dillingham, 1916); *My Aunt Angie* (New York: Farrar & Rinehart, 1930); *My Uncle Oswald* (New York: Farrar & Rinehart, 1931); Epes Winthrop Sargent, 'The Literary Side of Pictures', 199.

30. Jacobs, 22.

31. Jacobs, 25, including a reproduction of the scenario.

32. Jacobs, 27–28; a variant is reproduced in George C. Pratt, *Spellbound in Darkness: A History of the Silent Film*, rev. edn. (Greenwich, Conn. New York Graphic Society, 1973), 24–25.

33. Jacobs, 38–46; Pratt, 29–37. The text of *American Fireman* has been the subject of scholarly investigation as the result of the appearance of two different versions of the film. See Andre Gaudreault, 'Detours in Film Narrative: Crosscutting', *Cinema Journal* 19, no. 1 (Fall 1979). The discussion of the film here does not depend on the differences between the two versions.

34. Jacobs, 36–37.

35. Niver, 30.

36. Edwin S. Porter, 'Evolution of the Motion Picture', *Moving Picture World*, 21 (11 July 1914): 206; reprinted in Geduld, 35.

37. Ramsaye, 417.

38. D.J. Wenden, *The Birth of the Movies* (New York: E.P. Dutton, 1975), 21. Charles Musser, *Before the Nickelodeon: Edwin S. Porter and the Edison Manufacturing Co.* (Berkeley: University of California Press, 1991): 256–259.

39. Vardac, 182; for an account of popularity, see George C. Pratt, 'No Magic, No Mystery, No Sleight of Hand', reprinted in Tino Balio, ed., *The American Film Industry* (Madison: University of Wisconsin Press, 1976), 58; for critical comment, see Jacobs, 35–51; Pratt, *Spellbound in Darkness*, 32–33; Karel Reisz, *The Technique of Film Editing*, 2nd edn. (London: Focal Press, 1968), 16–20; and John L. Fell, *A History of Films* (New York: Holt, Rinehart and Winston, 1979), 45–47.

40. George Blaisdell, 'Edwin S. Porter', *Moving Picture World*, 14 (7 December 1912): 962.

41. Porter in Geduld, 34.

42. It would be much more helpful to view Porter's works in light of the French critical term 'decoupage', meaning all narrative segmentation and arrangement, taking place during writing, production, and/or editing. For an excellent discussion of the nuances of 'decoupage', see Noel Burch, *Theory of Film Practice*, trans. Helen R. Lane (New York: Praeger, 1973), 3–16.

43. Rachel Low and Roger Manvell, *The History of the British Film 1896–1906* (London: Allen & Unwin, 1948), 108.

44. Cecil Hepworth, 'Those Were the Days', *Penguin Film Review*, no. 6 (April 1948), 33–39; reprinted in Geduld, 29.

45. Richard Arlo Sanderson, 'A Historical Study of the Development of American Motion Picture Content and Techniques Prior to 1904', Diss. University of Southern California 1961, 119.

46. Robert Clyde Allen, 'Vaudeville and Film 1895–1915: A Study in Media Interaction', Diss. The University of Iowa 1977, 151, 212. See also Tom Gunning, 'The Cinema of Attractions: Early Film, Its Spectators and the Avant-Garde' in Thomas Elsaesser, ed., *Early Cinema: Space Frame Narrative* (London: BFI Publishing, 1990), 56. Charles Musser's study of the Edison Manufacturing Co. reveals a different set of statistics in which the percentages of actualities and fictional films fluctuate back and forth between August 1904 and February 1907. First fiction films dominate (62 to 38 per cent) then actualities (69 to 31 per cent) then fiction films (52 to 48 per cent) then actualities (80 to 20 per cent). See Musser's *Before the Nickelodeon*, 282–284.

47. Ramsaye, 414.

48. Hampton, 44.

49.   Jacobs, 52.

50.   Allen, 157, 217–220.

51.   Alfred A. Cohn, 'The Author Gets His', *Photoplay*, (February 1918): 80; Ramsaye, 653–654.

52.   Ramsaye, 453; Robert M. Henderson, *D.W. Griffith: The Years at Biograph* (New York: Farrar, Straus and Giroux, 1970), 29.

53.   Writing credits, necessarily tentative in this period, listed throughout this work are compiled from the following sources: *Catalog of Copyright Entries: Motion Pictures 1912–1939* (Washington, DC: Copyright Office, The Library of Congress, 1951); *Wid's Year Book, 1918–1921/22* (New York: Wid's Films and Film Folks, 1918–1921); *The Film Daily Yearbook, 1922/23–1936* (New York: Film Daily, 1922–1936); *Motion Picture Studio Directory and Trade Annual, 1918–1923/24* (Chicago Motion Picture News, 1918–1923); Kenneth W. Munden, exec. ed., *The American Film Institute Catalogue of Motion Pictures Produced in the United States, Part I: Feature Films 1921/1930*, 2 vols (New York: Bowker, 1970); *The American Film Institute Catalogue: Feature Films, 1911–1920*, ed. Patricia King Hanson (Berkeley: University of California Press, 1988); and Leonard Spigelgass, ed., *Who Wrote the Movie and What Else Did He Write? An Index of Screen Writers and Their Film Works 1936–69* (Los Angeles: AMPAS & Writers Guild, west, 1970).

54.   Anthony Slide, *Aspects of American Film History Prior to 1920* (Metuchen, NJ: Scarecrow Press, 1978), 87–96.

55.   Epes Winthrop Sargent, 'The Ben Hur Case', *Moving Picture World* (10 December 1911): 793; Ramsaye, 462–463.

56.   Jacobs, 52–66; Hampton, 46. See also Janet Staiger, 'The Division of Production: the Subdivision of the Work from the First Years through the 1920s' in David Bordwell, Janet Staiger, and Kristin Thompson, *The Classical Hollywood Cinema: Film Style and Mode of Production to 1960* (New York: Columbia University Press, 1985), 142–153.

57.   Clifford Howard, 'The Cinema in Retrospect', Pt. II, *Close Up* (London: December 1928), 31–32.

58.   Howard, 'The Cinema in Retrospect', Pts. I & II (November 1928), 16–25; (December 1928), 31–41.

59.   R.V.S., 'Scenario Construction', *Moving Picture World*, 8 (11 February 1911): 294.

60.   Lloyd Lonergan, 'How I Came To Write "Conti-nuity"', *Moving Picture World*, 33 (21 July 1917): 403 .

61.   John W. Kellette, 'Makers of the Movies: The Loner-gans', *Moving Picture World*, 21 (12 September 1914): 1497; Epes Winthrop Sargent, 'The Literary Side of Pictures', 199; Smith, 330.

62.   Macgowan, 350 .

63.   Eustace Hale Ball, *Photoplay Scenarios: How To Write and Sell Them* (New York: Hearst's International Library, 1915), 69.

64.   Ruth Wing, ed., *The Blue Book of the Screen* (Hollywood: Blue Book, 1923), 355; *New York Times* (2 May 1939), 23 (obituary).

65.   Mrs D.W. Griffith (Linda Arvidson), *When the Movies Were Young* (1925; rpt. New York: Dover, 1969), 62–66 ; Jacobs, 134 ; Slide, 99.

66.   Frank E. Woods, 'Functions of the Editorial Department', in *Opportunities in the Motion Picture Industry*, 20; Griffith, 65.

67.   Griffith, 245–251;

68.   Russell Merritt, 'Dixon, Griffith, and the Southern Legend', *Cinema Journal*, 12, no. 1 (Fall 1972): 26–37.

69.   *New York Times*, (2 May 1939), 23 (obituary); Epes Winthrop Sargent, 'The Literary Side of Pictures', 201.

70.   Smith, 330; Griffith, 64–65.

71.   Emmett Campbell Hall, 'Some Scenarios – and Others', *Moving Picture World*, 9 (22 July 1911), 109; Robert Grau, *The Stage in the Twentieth Century* (New York: Broadway, 1912), 85–86; Smith, 330; Epes Winthrop Sargent, 'The Literary Side of Pictures', 200.

72.   Ruth Wing, 350.

73.   Smith, 330; Ruth Wing, 350; husband/wife screen-writing teams in the sound era would include Frances Goodrich and Albert Hackett, Dorothy Parker and Alan Campbell, Henry and Phoebe Ephron, Ruth Gordon and Garson Kanin, Fay and Michael Kanin, and Joan Didion an John Gregory Dunne.

74.   Ramsaye, 509–510; Henderson, *D.W. Griffith: The Years at Biograph*, 241–242.

75.   Robert M. Henderson, *D. W. Griffith: His Life and Work* (New York: Oxford University Press, 1972), 35–36.

76.   Kenneth Macgowan, 'The March of the Photoplay', *Motion Picture Classic* (May 1919), 71, 80.

77. Smith, 327.

78. Macpherson, 28.

79. 'Giving Credit Where Credit Is Due', *Moving Picture World*, 6 (12 March 1910): 369–370.

80. Hampton, 64–82.

81. Hampton, 83–100; Tino Balio, *United Artists: The Company Built By the Stars* (Madison: University of Wisconsin Press, 1976), 3–29.

82. W. Stephen Bush, 'Do Longer Films Make Better Show?' *Moving Picture World*, 10 (28 October 1911): 275.

83. Jacobs, 90–94; Hampton, 101–120.

84. Epes Winthrop Sargent, 'Advertising for Exhibitors', *Moving Picture World*, 15 (24 February 1913): 666.

85. Jacobs, 129–130; *Biograph Bulletins 1896–1908*, comp. Kemp R. Niver, ed. Bebe Bergsten (Los Angeles: Locare Research Group, 1971), 24; 'Technique and the Tale', *Moving Picture World*, 10 (18 November 1911): 541; Epes Winthrop Sargent, 'The Literary Side of Pictures', 201; Hampton, 207–208; Epes Winthrop Sargent, *The Technique of the Photoplay*, 2nd edn. (New York: Chalmers, 1913), 9.

86. Emma Worcester Sargent and Charles Sprague Sargent, *Epes Sargent of Gloucester and His Descendants*, edition limited to 500 copies (Boston: Houghton Mifflin, 1923), 291–292.

87. John F. Barry and Epes W. Sargent, *Building Theater Patronage: Management and Merchandising* (New York: Chalmers, 1927), preface, n.p.; *New York Times* (8 December 1938), 27 (obituary).

88. Douglas Gilbert, *American Vaudeville: Its Life and Times* 1940; rpt. (New York: Dover, 1963), 152–153.

89. *New York Times*, (8 December 1938), 27.

90. Gilbert, 153.

91. Abel Green and Joe Laurie, Jr., *Show Biz: From Vaude to Video* (New York: Henry Holt, 1951). Sargent is mentioned twice, 49, 108, both in cursory fashion; Gilbert, 155.

92. See Allen for an excellent discussion of vaudeville/film interaction.

93. Epes Winthrop Sargent, 'The Literary Side of Pictures', 200, 202; Smith, 328. As copyright entries prior to 1912 list only the producer, Sargent's writing credits are obscured. However, subsequent entries indicate that from 1913 to 1916 Sargent wrote 49 films, all but two split- or one-reelers for Lubin, many directed by Arthur W. Hotaling.

94. 'A List of Publications of the Descendants of Epes Sargent', comp. Julia M. Johnson, in Emma Worcester Sargent and Charles Sprague Sargent, *Sargent of Gloucester and His Descendants*, 33–34.

95. A.W. Thomas, 'The Photoplaywright and His Art', *Photoplay* (August 1912): 88.

96. Jacobs.

A Bibliography

Books

American Motion Picture Directory, 1914–15 (Chicago: American Motion Picture Directory Co., 1915).

Balio, Tino, ed. *The American Film Industry* (Madison: Univ. of Wisconsin Press, 1976).

Ball, Eustace Hale. *Photoplay Scenarios: How To Write and Sell Them* (New York: Hearst's International Library, 1915).

Balshofer, Fred J., and Arthur C. Miller. *One Reel a Week* (Berkeley: Univ. of California Press, 1967).

Barker, E.F. *The Art of Photoplay Writing* (St. Louis: Colossus, 1917).

Barry, John F., and Epes W. Sargent. *Building Theater Patronage: Management and Merchandising* (New York. Chalmers, 1927).

Bertsch, Marguerite. *How To Write for Moving Pictures* (New York: George H. Doran, 1917).

Biograph Bulletins 1896–1908. Comp. Kemp R. Niver, ed. Bebe Bergsten (Los Angeles: Locare Research Group, 1971).

Brewer Terry. *Kops and Custards: The Legend of Keystone Films* (Norman: Univ. of Oklahoma Press, 1968).

Brownlow, Kevin. *The Parade's Gone By* (New York: Knopf, 1968).

Carr, Catherine. *The Art of Photoplay Writing* (New York: Hannis Jordan, 1914.)

Catalog of Copyright Entries: Motion Pictures 1912–1939 (Washington, DC: Copyright Office, The Library of Congress, 1951).

Cinema Catalogue: Larry Edmunds Bookshop, Inc. (Hollywood: Larry Edmunds Bookshop, n.d.).

Corliss, Richard, ed. *The Hollywood Screenwriters* (New York : Avon, 1972). *Talking Pictures: Screen-*

writers in the American Cinema 1927–1973 (Woodstock, NY: Overlook Press, 1974).

Couperie, Pierre, et al. *A History of the Comic Strip.* Trans. Eileen B. Hennessy (New York: Crown, 1968).

De Mille, Agnes. *Dance to the Piper* (Boston:Atlantic-Little, Brown, 1952).

DeMille, Cecil B. *The Autobiography of Cecil B. DeMille*, ed. Donald Hayne (Englewood Cliffs, NJ: Prentice-Hall, 1959).

De Mille, William. *Hollywood Saga* (New York: Dutton, 1939).

Dimick, Howard T. *Modern Photoplay Writing* (Franklin, Ohio: James Knapp Reeve, 1922).

Edmonds, I. G. *Big U: Universal in the Silent Days* (New York: A.S. Barnes, 1977).

Emerson, John, and Anita Loos. *How To Write Photoplays* (New York: McCann, 1920).

Esenwein, J. Berg, and Arthur Leeds. *Writing the Photoplay* (Springfield, Mass.: Home Correspondence School, 1913).

The Film Daily Yearbook, 1922/23–1936 (New York: Film Daily, 1922–1936).

Fowler, Gene. *Father Goose* (New York: Crown, 1934).

Fox, Charles Donald, and Milton L. Silver, eds. *Who's Who on the Screen* (New York: Ross, 1920).

Freeburg, Victor Oscar. *The Art of Photoplay Making.* 1918; rpt. (New York: Arno Press, 1970). *Disguise Plots in Elizabethan Drama: A Study in Stage Tradition* (New York: Columbia Univ. Press, 1915). *Pictorial Beauty on the Screen.* (1923; rpt. New York: Arno Press,1970).

Freytag, Gustav. *Technique of the Drama*, trans. Elias J. MacEwan (Chicago: Griggs, 1898).

Froug, William. *The Screenwriter Looks at the Screenwriter* (New York: Macmillan, 1972).

Gilbert, Douglas. *American Vaudeville: Its Life and Times* (1940; rpt. New York: Dover, 1963).

Grau, Robert. *The Stage in the Twentieth Century* (New York: Broadway, 1912). *The Theatre of Science* (New York; Broadway, 1914).

Green, Abel, and Joe Laurie, Jr. *Show Biz: From Vaude to Video* (New York: Henry Holt, 1951).

Griffith, Mrs D.W. (Linda Arvidson). *When the Movies Were Young* (1925; rpt. New York: Dover, 1969).

Hampton, Benjamin B. *History of the American Film Industry from Its Beginnings to 1931;* (Rpt. New York: Dover, 1970).

Harrison, Louis Reeves. *Screencraft* (New York: Chalmers, 1916).

Hart, William S. *My Life East and West,* 1929; (Rpt. Bronx, NY: Benjamin Blom, 1968).

Higham, Charles. *Cecil B. DeMille* (New York: Scribner's, 1973).

Hoagland, Herbert Case. *How To Write a Photoplay* (New York: Magazine Maker, 1912).

Irwin, Will. *The House that Shadows Built* (Garden City, NY: Doubleday, Doran & Co., 1928).

Jacobs, Lewis. *The Rise of the American Film: A Critical History.* (1939; rpt. New York: Teachers College Press, 1968).

Koszarski, Diane Kaiser. *The Complete Films of William S. Hart: A Pictorial Record* (New York: Dover, 1980).

Lahue, Kalton C. *Continued Next Week: A History of the Moving Picture Seria* (Norman: Univ. of Oklahoma Press, 1964). *Dreams for Sale: The Rise and Fall of the Triangle Film Corporation.* (New York: A. S. Barnes, 1971).

Lane, Tamar. *The New Technique of Screenwriting* (New York: McGraw-Hill,1936).

Lasky, Jesse L. *I Blow My Own Horn.* With Don Weldon (Garden City: Doubleday, 1957).

Lasky, Jesse L., Jr. *What Ever Happened to Hollywood?* (New York: Funk & Wagnalls, 1975).

Latham, Aaron. *Crazy Sundays: F. Scott Fitzgerald in Hollywood* (New York: Viking, 1971).

Lawson, John Howard. *Film: The Creative Process* 2nd ed. (New York: Hill & Wang, 1967). *Theory and Technique of Playwriting and Screenwriting* (New York: Putnam's, 1949).

Lindsay, Vachel. *The Art of the Moving Picture.* 2nd ed. Intro. by Stanley Kauffmann (1922; rpt. New York: Liveright, 1970).

Loos, Anita. *A Girl Like I* (New York: Viking, 1966). *Kiss Hollywood Goodbye* (New York: Viking, 1974).

Lowrey, Carolyn. *The First Hundred Noted Men and Women of the Screen* (New York: Moffat, Yard, and Co., 1920).

Lyons, Timothy James. *The Silent Partner: The History of the American Film Manufacturing Company 1910–1921* (New York: Arno Press, 1974).

Macgowan, Kenneth. *Behind the Screen: The History and Technique of the Motion Picture* (New York: Delacorte, 1965).

Marion, Frances. *How To Write and Sell Film Stories* (New York: Covici-Friede, 1937). *Off With Their Heads: A Serio-Comic Tale of Hollywood* (New York: Macmillan, 1972).

McCardell, Roy L. *Conversations of a Chorus Girl* (New York: Street & Smith, 1903).*The Diamond from the Sky* (New York: G. W. Dillingham, 1916). *Jimmy Jones: The Autobiography of an Office Boy* (Boston: Dana Estes, 1907). *My Aunt Angie* (New York: Farrar & Rinehart, 1930). *My Uncle Oswald* (New York: Farrar & Rinehart, 1931). *Olde Love and Lavender & Other Verses* (New York: Godfrey A.S. Wieners, 1900). *The Show Girl and Her Friends* (New York: Street & Smith, 1904). *The Wage Slaves of New York* (New York: G.W. Dillingham, 1899).

McLaughlin, Robert. *Broadway and Hollywood: A History of Economic Interaction* (New York: Arno Press, 1974).

Motion Picture Almanac, 1931, (New York: Quigley Publications, 1931).

Motion Picture Studio Directory and Trade Annual, 1918–1923/24 (Chicago: Motion Picture News, 1918–23).

Munden, Kenneth W. (exec. ed.) *The American Film Institute Catalogue of Motion Pictures Produced in the United States, Part I: Feature Films 1921/1930,* 2 vols, (New York: Bowker, 1970).

Munsterberg, Hugo. *The Film: A Psychological Study.* Foreward by Richard Griffith (1916; rpt. New York: Dover, 1970).

Niver, Kemp R. *The First Twenty Years: A Segment of Film History* (Los Angeles: Artisan Press, 1968).

North, Joseph H. *The Early Development of the Motion Picture (1887–1909)* (New York: Arno Press, 1973).

Pagel, Raoul. *Hollywood Film Production Manual* (Burbank, Calif.: Raoul Pagel, 1976).

Parsons, Louella O. *How To Write for the 'Movies',* rev. edn. (Chicago: A. C. McClurg, 1917).

Patterson, Frances Taylor. *Cinema Craftsmanship* (New York: Harcourt, Brace and Howe, 1920). *Scenario and Screen* (New York: Harcourt, Brace, 1928).

Peacocke, Captain Leslie T. *Hints on Photoplay Writing* (Chicago: Photoplay Publishing, 1916).

Phillips, Henry Albert. *The Photodrama* (Larchmont: Stanhope-Dodge, 1914).

Pratt, George C. *Spellbound in Darkness: A History of the Silent Film,* rev. edn. (Greenwich, Conn.: New York Graphic Society, 1973).

Ramsaye, Terry. *A Million and One Nights: A History of the Motion Picture* (New York: Simon & Schuster, 1926).

Ross, Lillian. *Picture* (1952; rpt. New York: Avon, 1969).

Rowlands, Avril. *Script Continuity and the Production Secretary in Film and TV* (New York: Hastings House, 1977).

Sadoul, Georges. *Dictionary of Film Makers.* Trans., ed., & updated Peter Morris (Berkeley: Univ. of California Press, 1972).

Sargent, Emma Worcester, and Charles Sprague Sargent. *Epes Sargent of Gloucester and His Descendants,* limited edn. (Boston: Houghton Mifflin, 1923).

Sargent, Epes Winthrop. *Technique of the Photoplay* (New York: Chalmers, 1912). *Technique of the Photoplay,* 2nd edn. (New York: Chalmers, 1913). *Technique of the Photoplay,* 3rd edn. (New York: Chalmers, 1916).

Slevin, James. *On Picture-Play Writing: A Handbook of Workmanship* (Cedar Grove, NJ: Farmer Smith, 1912).

Slide, Anthony. *Aspects of American Film History Prior to 1920* (Metuchen, NJ: Scarecrow Press, 1978). *Early American Cinema* (New York: A.S. Barnes, 1970).

Spigelgass, Leonard, ed. *Who Wrote the Movie and What Else Did He Write? An Index of Screen Writers and Their Film Works 1936–69* (Los Angeles: A.M.P.A.S. & Writers Guild, west, 1970).

Talbot, Frederick A. *Moving Pictures: How They Are Made and Worked* (Philadelphia: Lippincott, 1912).

Thomas, A.W. *How To Write a Photoplay* (Chicago: Photoplaywrights Assoc. of America, 1914).

Thomas, Bob. *Thalberg: Life and Legend* (New York: Doubleday, 1969).

Van Loan, H.H. *How I Did It* (Los Angeles: Whittingham Press, 1922).

Vardac, A. Nicholas. *Stage to Screen: Theatrical Methods from Garrick to Griffith* (Cambridge: Harvard Univ. Press, 1949).

Vincent, Carl, Ricardo Redi, and Franco Venturini,

eds. *General Bibliography of the Motion Pictures* (1953; rpt. New York: Arno Press, 1972).

Wescott, Harry D. *A Glossary for the Students of the Stanley V. Mastbaum Course in Photoplay Study and Scenario Writing at Temple University and the Course at New York University* (New York: n.p., 1921).

Wid's Year Book, 1918–1921/22 (New York: Wid's Films and Film Folks, 1918–21).

Wolfe, Glen Joseph. *Vachel Lindsay: The Poet as Film Theorist* (New York: Arno Press, 1973).

Wright, William Lord. *Photoplay Writing* (New York: Falk, 1922).

Articles and periodicals

Bartlett, Randolph. 'A Boy Named Kelly', *Photoplay* (April 1917): 83–84, 152.

Bodeen, Dewitt. 'Frances Marion', Pts. I & II. *Films in Review* (February 1969): 71–91; (March 1969): 129–152.

Bush, W. Stephen. 'Do Longer Films Make Better Show?' *Moving Picture World*, 10 (28 October 1911): 275. 'Interview with Edwin Milton Royle'. *Moving Picture World*, 19 (21 February 1914): 930.

Carr, Harry C. 'What Next?' *Photoplay* (March 1917): 60–63, 146.

Clarke, T.E.B. 'Screenwriter and Director in a British Studio', *Screen Writer* (June 1947): 14–16.

Cohn, Alfred A. 'The Author Gets His', *Photoplay* (February 1918): 79–80, 122. 'A Sunlight Dumas: C. Gardner Sullivan, the Speed-and-Power King of Authorial Inceville', *Photoplay* (May 1916): 147–49.

'The Confessions of a Scenario Editor', *Photoplay* (August 1914): 164–168.

Deutelbaum, Marshall. 'Structural Patterning in the Lumiere Films', *Wide Angle*, 3, no. 1 (1978): 28–37.

Eaton, Walter Prichard. 'Wanted – Motion Picture Authors', *American Magazine* (March 1916): 34, 67–67.

'Editors and Authors Organise New Club', *Photoplay Author*, 2 (December 1913): 172.

Eisenstein, Sergei. 'On the Form of the Scenario', Abridged and trans. as 'A Russian View of Scenarios', *New York Times* (30 March 1939): Sec. 8, 3.

'Famous Authors with Universal', *Moving Picture World*, 21 (5 September 1914): 1356.

Giffen, R. L. 'The Prussian Authocracy', *Photoplay* (April 1919): 30, 98–99.

'Giving Credit Where Credit Is Due', *Moving Picture World*, 6 (12 March 1910): 369–370.

Hall, Emmett Campbell. 'Some Scenarios – and Others', *Moving Picture World*, 9 (22 July 1911): 109.

Hamilton, Clayton. 'The Art of the Moving Picture Play', *Bookman*, 32 (January 1911): 512–516.

Hepworth, Cecil. 'Those Were the Days'. *Penguin Film Review*, no. 6 (April 1948): 33–39.

'How Twelve Famous Women Scenario Writers Succeeded', *Photoplay* (August 1923): 31–33.

Howard, Clifford. 'The Cinema in Retrospect', Pts. I & II. *Close-Up* (London: November 1928): 16–25 (December 1928): 31–41.

Ince, Thomas H. 'The Undergraduate and the Scenario', *Bookman*, 47 (June 1918): 415–418.

Jones, Marc Edmund. 'The Photoplay Forum', *Photoplay* (September 1913): 106–108.

Jones, Marc Edmund and others, 'The Photoplaywrights' Department', *Photoplay* (1912–1916).

Katterjohn, Monte M. 'Thumbnail Biographies: Richard V. Spencer of Kay-Bee, Broncho, and Domino', *Photoplay* (November 1914): 168.

Kellette, John W. 'Makers of the Movies: The Lonergans', *Moving Picture World*, 21 (12 September 1914): 1497–1498.

Lang, Phil. 'The Scenario of Today', *Moving Picture World*, 33 (21 July 1917): 406–07.

Leeds, Arthur. 'Thinks and Things', *Writer's Monthly*, 7 (January 1916): 31. 'Thinks and Things', *Writer's Monthly*, 8 (November-December 1916): 209.

Lonergan, Lloyd. 'How I Came To Write Continuity', *Moving Picture World*, 33 (21 July 1917): 403.

Lowe, Edward T. 'Ideals and Realities', *Moving Picture World*, 33 (21 July 1917): 407.

'Lumière – The Last Interview', *Sight and Sound*, 17 (Summer 1948): 68–70.

Macgowan, Kenneth. 'The March of the Photoplay', *Motion Picture Classic* (May 1919): 16–17, 71–80.

Macpherson, Jeanie. 'Functions of the Continuity Writer', In *Opportunities in the Motion Picture In-*

dustry, (Los Angeles: Photoplay Research Society, 1922): 25–35.

Martin, Alice. 'From "Wop" Parts to Bossing the Job', *Photoplay* (October 1916): 95–97.

Mathis, June. 'Tapping the Thought Wireless', *Moving Picture World*, 33 (21 July 1917): 409.

McQuade, James J. 'James Oliver Curwood', *Moving Picture World*, 21 (5 September 1914): 1352–1353.

Merritt, Russell. 'Dixon, Griffith, and the Southern Legend', *Cinema Journal*, 12, no. 1 (Fall 1972): 26–37.

Nichols, Dudley. 'The Writer and the Film', In *Great Film Plays*. Ed. John Gassner and Dudley Nichols (New York: Crown, 1959): IX–XVII.

'Noted Dramatists to Write Moving Picture Plays', *Moving Picture World*, 2 (28 March 1908): 263.

'On the Photoplay Serial: An Interview with Eustace Hale Ball', *The Editor*, 45 (April 1917): 294–296.

'$1,000 for an Idea! The Thomas H. Ince – Photoplay Magazine Scenario Contest', *Photoplay* (September 1916): 46.

Peltret, Elizabeth. 'Frances Marion – Soldieress of Fortune', Porter, Edwin S. 'Evolution of the Motion Picture', *Moving Picture World*, 21 (11 July 1914): 206.

Pratt, George. 'No Magic, No Mystery, No Slight of Hand', Reprinted in Balio, op. cit., 46–58.

S., R.V. 'Scenario Construction' *Moving Picture World*, 8 (11 February 1911): 294.

Sargent, Epes Winthrop. 'Advertising fo Exhibitors', *Moving Picture World*, 15 (24 February 1913): 666. 'The Ben Hur Case', *Moving Picture World*, 10 (9 December 1911): 793. 'The Literary Side of Pictures', *Moving Picture World*, 21 (11 July 1914): 199–202. 'Progress in Photoplay Writing', In *Motion Picture Annual and Yearbook for 1912* (New York: Moving Picture World, 1913): 18–22. 'The Photoplaywright', *Moving Picture World* (1 June 1912–12 July 1919). 'Technique of the Photoplay', *Moving Picture World* (22 July 1911–9 September 1911). [Gorenflot]. 'Thinks and Things', *Photoplay Author* (becomes *Writer's Monthly*): 1912–18. 'The Scenario Writer'. *Moving Picture World* (16 December 1911–30 March 1912).

'The Scenario', *Moving Picture World*, 7 (23 September 1910), 679.

'Scenarios They Want', *Photoplay* (July 1916, 79–83).

Schmidt, Karl. 'The Handwriting on the Screen', *Everybody's*, 36 (May 1917): 622–623.

Simonov, Konstantin. 'The Soviet Film Industry', *Screen Writer*, 2 (June 1946): 17–30.

'The Sinews of War'. New York *Dramatic News* (26 March 1913): 25.

Smith, Russell E. 'The Authors of the Photoplay', *Book News Monthly*, 33 (March 1915): 326–332.

Staiger, Janet. 'Dividing Labour for Production Control: Thomas Ince and the Rise of the Studio System', *Cinema Journal*, 17, no. 2 (Spring 1979): 16–25.

Steck, H. Tipton. 'Doing My Bit', *Moving Picture World*, 33 (21 July 1917): 408–09.

Sterne, Elaine. 'Writing for the Movies as a Profession', *Photoplay* (October 1914): 156, 158.

'Studio Directory'. *Motion Picture News* (21 October 1916): 128–137 (12 April 1917): 155–164.

'Technique and the Tale'. *Moving Picture World*, 10 (18 November 1911): 541.

Thomas, Arthur W. 'The Photoplaywright and His Art'. *Photoplay* (February 1913): 120–123; (August 1913): 84–85.

Van Rensselaer, Alexander. 'Photoplay Writing and the Photoplay Market', *Bookman*, 56 (November 1922): 299–304.

Wing, William E. 'Tom Ince of Inceville', New York *Dramatic Mirror* (24 December 1913): 34.

Woods, Frank E. 'Function of the Editorial Department', In *Opportunities in the Motion Picture Industry* (Los Angeles: Photoplay Research Society, 1922), 19–23.

Other sources

Aitken Brothers' Papers. Wisconsin Centre for Theatre Research, Univ. of Wisconsin-Madison.

Allen, Robert Clyde. 'Vaudeville and Film 1895–1915: A Study in Media Interaction'. Diss. The Univ. of Iowa 1977.

Thomas H. Ince Collection. Library of Congress, Washington, DC.

Sanderson, Richard Arlo. 'A Historical Study of the Development of American Motion Picture Content and Techniques Prior to 1904'. Diss. Univ. of Southern California 1961.

Film History, Volume 9, pp. 257–268, 1997. Copyright © John Libbey & Company
ISSN: 0892-2160. Printed in Australia

Written scenarios of early French cinema: screenwriting practices in the first twenty years

Isabelle Raynauld

The study of screenwriting practices – especially those of the pre-1914 period – has significantly changed over the last decade. The film script is now an integral part of film studies,[1] yet only ten years ago, when I first began my research on early cinema screenplays, historians and non-historians alike still considered that, as a rule, improvisation prevailed and that in fact no screenplays were written during these first years of cinema. This article summarises the results of over a decade of research conducted in French archives, namely at the Bibliothèque Nationale in Paris, where I discovered that no fewer than 10,000 screenplays were registered from 1907 through 1923. These screenplays are now kept at the Bibliothèque de l'Arsenal in Paris. This article will clearly establish the status of these texts, which have for too long been considered as mere advertisements, and will put forth a historical as well as a narratological analysis of the first French screenplays.[2]

The 1990 Domitor symposium held in Quebec City gave us the opportunity to put forth a number of observations pertaining to the screenwriting practices that prevailed prior to 1914.[3] Here we will examine a wide range of types of screenplays and use these to describe the first step in the conception of a film: its mapping out in the form of a script. After reviewing different examples of manuscripts written before 1914, we will observe the progression of narrative construction and storytelling as it was devised and/or transformed for filmmaking purposes.

The diversity of the forms of existing texts suggests how very quickly the practice of this new form of writing developed and established itself.

The screenplays under examination here come from French and American archival collections and offer a convincing array of the types of screenplays that abounded during the first years of cinema. Each text presents different stages in the scenario's devel-

Isabelle Raynauld is an Assistant Professor of Film at the University of Montreal. Author of more than twenty articles and book chapters, she has co-edited special issues of *Iris* and *Etudes Litteraires* and presented papers on the screenplay at numerous international conferences. Address correspondence to the Department of Art History , University of Montreal, C.P. 6128, succursale Centre-ville, Montreal, Quebec, Canada H3C 3J7.

Fig. 1. A sample 'A' category script: page one of the four-page script for *Le bonhomme Noël* (1907). The screenplay is not accompanied by a filmstrip.

logues. Therefore, any single title may have been given more than one date and copyright registration number. Each copyright marks a different step in the development of the text. We will also see that several versions of the same screenplay exist. Close analysis of the various texts will enable us to clearly distinguish the differences between the screenplay written prior to the film's production and the text registered after the film was actually produced. Moreover, these texts will reveal that techniques of montage, of continuity editing and of narrative inventiveness were at the forefront of the screenwriters' preoccupations, even in cinema's early years.

Categories of the registered text

Screenplays registered at the Bibliothèque de l'Arsenal were registered and deposited either with or without a corresponding filmstrip stapled to the page. Our research aimed to discover if more than one version of a screenplay existed under the same title, and to verify if indeed there could be more than one copyright for a single title. As a result of this, it was possible to establish a chronology of different variations and versions of the texts under the same title.

First category: 'A' versions

The first category we have established is that of single-version screenplays without a filmstrip accompanying the *manuscript*. These are dated for the most part from 1907. We have named them 'A' versions. A good example of this category of texts is *Le bonhomme Noël*, Gaumont 1907, which is four pages in length. It is referred to as '*scénario de scène cinématographique*', or script consisting of film scenes. It is one of Gaumont's very first registrations although, quite exceptionally, it has no copyright number.

The length of these texts range from one to three or four pages. Each screenplay is divided into tableaux or scenes, each corresponding to a differ-

opment. Some of the texts kept at the Bibliothèque Nationale are summaries written after the films' completion, but a good number of them are without a doubt screenplays written before the films were shot. Contemporary screenwriters still write their scripts before the film is shot, and, like their predecessors in early cinema, they still write many more screenplays than actual films are made.

The screenplays presented here range from the first draft written before the film was made up to a 'final draft', a summary of the completed film as it was published in the production companies' cata-

ent space. The number of the tableau and the indication of the space in which the action is set are followed by a description of the action, written in the present tense.

Another example of a version A screenplay, usually brief, but very representative of the screenplays of the time, is that of *Pincés*, Gaumont 1907, copyright #4644. The screenplay fits a single page and is divided into four tableaux, each corresponding to a different space and time. The story, designed for a 100 metre spool of film, is complete, with a beginning, a middle and an end.

Later we will look at specific details of certain texts. We should point out that the registration dates do not automatically correspond to the moment the texts were written, since it was common practice to have them registered in bulk, not when they were produced. Therefore, a more recent text may have the same copyright registration date as another written several months earlier. Of course, a text cannot have been written after its registration date.

IMPRIME PAR PATHE FRERES
Compagnie générale de Phonographes Cinématographes et Appareils de Précision - Siège Social : 98 Rue de Richelieu- PARIS.

NOEL DU MISEREUX.

I. Dépôt conforme à la vue.

Dans une mansarde , trois enfants sont assis à une table , qui avec le lit et deux chaises forment l'unique mobilier des pauvres gens.
Le père arrive avec un pain ; aussitôt tous les enfants se précipitent vers lui , affamés . Le père le coupe en quatre et aussitôt tous mangent ou plutôt dévorent leur misérable morceau de pain , assis autour de la table où [illegible] manque la place de la mère de famille est vide .- Mais une vision apparait : La mère des enfants avec un ange contemplent lesorphelins et les bénit , puis disparait -
Mais c'est cette nuit que le père Noël doit venir apporter de beaux jouets aux enfants bien sages ; le père des pauvres petits y songe et emmène les enfants se promener un peu dans les rues .

II.

Il neige à gros flocons ... succombant de fatigue et de faim , les malheureux arrivent , voient un banc et s'y asseoient , puis , harassés , finissent par s'endormir sous la neige qui tombe de plus en plus drue .- Au-dessous de la famille endormie et derrière le banc apparait une vision d'anges qui bénit la famille et leur promet des jours meilleurs , puis la vision disparait .- Les pauvres petits songent ... au loin , le père Noël vient vers eux , avec sa grosse hotte sur le dos , chargée de beaux jouets , [illegible] ; alors , le père des petits veut des jouets pour ses enfants , il se précipite vers le père Noël ... qui , hélás ! n'est qu'un brutal chiffonnier debout avant l'aurore , qui see croyant attaqué , frappe violemment le misérable qui tombe à terre , meurtri par les coups -
Cependant , les enfants ont appelé au secours : la grille de la propriété qui se trouve de ce côté de la rue et derrière le banc , s'ouvre , et des valets de chambre apparaissent ; ils transportent le malheureux dans la maison , les petits enfants suivent leur père .

III.

Intérieur de l'appartement - Dans un petit salon- La maitresse de maison envoie les enfants se réconforter et prépare une chaise pour le père .- On dépose celui-ci . La jeune femme lui bande la plaie qu'il a reçue au front , lui fait respirer des sels - Le malheureux revient à;lui et dit : " J'ai faim ! " Un domestique va chercher un bol de bouillon que l'on fait boire au misérable puis on le transporte dans une autre pièce ...

IV.

Cependant , ce soir , c'est fête dans la maison - On a réunis les amis des enfants de la maison , et au milieu du [illegible] salon brillamment éclairé s'élève un superbe arbre de Noël chargé de joujoux magnifiques . Les petits orphelins sont assis et contemplent avec de grands yeux naïfs toutes ces merveilles étalées devant eux et le luxe qui règne dans le salon - A ce moment on transporte le père au salon ; les petits orphelins se précipitent vers lui ; le père les embrasse - Puis on procède à la distribution des jouets - Les enfants ont chacun plusieurs jouets . les plus beaux : un beau cheval de bois .

Fig. 2. A sample of a 'B' category script: *Le Noël du misereux* (1907). The deposit conforms to the script.

We also discovered a number of more elaborate texts, such as *La perle noire*, (Pathé, 1907, three pages, copyright registration #3333) and *La policière*, (Pathé, 1907, four pages, copyright registration #3903), as well as *Le commissaire et les cambrioleurs*, (Gaumont, 1912, five pages, Library of Congress), submitted and registered in Washington by Alice Guy in 1912.

Second category: 'B' versions

The second category is *screenplays without an accompanying filmstrip and in several versions.* This category includes the 'A' versions, which have an earlier date of deposit, and the 'B' versions. The 'B' versions bear the notice 'deposit that conforms to the film'.[4] For example, there are two versions of *Le Noël du miséreux*: the 'A' version, *Le Noël du miséreux*, Pathé, 1907, one page, copyright registration

```
AU MULTICOPISTE                    8e SERIE

                                              PP 05590

              SCENES DRAMATIQUES


         LA PHOTOGRAPHIE ACCUSATRICE
                Produced by
             Thanhouser Company
           New Rochelle, New York

     Code télegr.                  Longueur....
     Ramonage                      N° 5590

         Le spéculateur Grenley s'aperçoit que l'attorney a des
charges contre lui. Pour échapper à l'arrestation qui le menace,
il décide d'acheter la complicité du représentant de la loi.
         Mais l'attorney n'a pas été seul à se montrer fin limier.
Son secrétaire , Roke est un homme de même calibre. Pendant l'entre-
vue que le spéculateur a eue avec l'attorney, le secrétaire indé-
licat, caché dans une pièce voisine, a réussi à prendre une photo -
graphie des plus compromettantes pour son patron. Il exerce dès
lors un chantage des plus profitables.
         Devenu paresseux et débauché, le secrétaire convoite la
femme de son ami Lovden . Un soir, se trouvant seul avec la jeune
femme, il risque une déclaration brutale. Elle se défend énergique-
ment. Le mari paraît à ce moment et se précipite sur l'intrus.
Dans la lutte, la lampe qui,seule éclairait la pièce ,s'éteint.
Un coup de feu, le bruit d'une chûte; : des policemen accourent,
rallument la lampe et découvrent à terre, le corps inanimé du
secrétaire. Mister Lovden, pour sauver sa femme,qu'il croit coupable
du meurtre, s'accuse à sa place. Mistress Lovden ,luttant de géné-
rosité avec son mari, s'accuse à son tour devant l'attorney, lors-
que paraît un témoin inattendu. C'est la servante /qui/la/ly/qr/qg/
du secrétaire assassiné, qui en accomplissant sa tâche journalière,
a découvert la photographie prouvant la complicité de l'attorney.
Lui seul était intéressé à la mort du secrétaire. Devant les
preuves qui l'accablent, le juge se trouble et avoue : Devenu à
moitié fou après les demandes réitérées du jeune secrétaire, il
l'a suivi , déterminé à en finir avec cette vie de tourments. /X/
d/X/qd/cXance/d/qr/XqXX//XX/ Par la fenêtre ouverte, il a vu
la scène se dérouler chez Lovden, ; profitant de l'obscurité soudaine,
il a tiré et s'est enfui, laissant la/XoxxqXX/ à l'innocent Lovden
la responsabilité de son crime.
```

Fig. 3. A sample of a 'C' category script: *La photographie accusatrice* (1912). The script is accompanied by a filmstrip and is written for subsequent publication in a sales catalogue.

#3767, and the 'B' version, *Le Noël du miséreux*, Pathé, 1908, one page, copyright registration #4208, which bears the notice 'deposit that conforms to the film'.

This notice, 'deposit that conforms to the film', characteristic of 'B' versions, is of great importance because the 'B' versions manifestly contain precise descriptions of actual elements to be found in the film, such as intertitles and *mise-en-scène* directions, which 'conform to the film'. The 'A' version is then the script written prior to the film, and the more elaborate and especially more precise 'B' version is the one that corresponds to the actual film. As well as being what could be called the shooting script and the revised version, the 'B' version also assures copyright protection of both initial subject, and final film.

In the case of *Noël du miséreux*, it is extremely interesting to compare the text of the first tableau of each version. Version 'A': 'In an attic, three children

IMPRIME PAR LA COMPAGNIE GENERALE DES ETABLISSEMENTS PATHE FRERES
Cinématographes - Phonographes - Capital 30 Millions de Frs .

C. DE MORLHON.—   Dépôt conftme à la vue .

P2246
sans photo.

LA BROYEUSE DE COEURS

Scène de la Vie cruelle par

M. C. de Morlhon.

PREMIERE PARTIE

PREMIER TABLEAU .-   L'inconstant .
Sous-Titre .- Pierre de Brézeux est fiancé à sa cousine Marthe Roxoy.—

Un salon.- Pierre et Marthe sont assis au salon et causent amicalement .
Pierre fait remarquer à sa cousine qu'il est bientôt l'heure de se retirer
Celle-ci lui fait " Oh. Déja ! " puis, se dirigeant vers la corbeille de
fleurs que Pierre lui a fait envoyer le soir même, en cueille une, qu'elle
embrasse avec amour, etvqu'elle place à son corsage . Pierre lui dit adieu
et sort; Marthe, seule, se dirige vers la fenêtre .

2e TABLEAU .- Premier plan du balcon.- Elle se penche au balcon et fait
adieu de la main . Puis elle rentre et tousse. Sa mère,qui rentre,lui repr
che de s'être dxposée au froid .

3e TABLEAU .- La porte de l'immeuble .- Sortie de Pierre qui salue sa
fiancée au balcon et part.

4e TABLEAU .- Le bureau de Pierre .- Rentré chez lui,il tend ses vêtements
à son domestique . Un groom lui porte unppli qu'il ouvre et lit .

PROJECTION.—   CERCLE ROYAL
          LE PRESIDENT .   Mon cher collègue,
            Vous êtes prié d'assister à la séan
            ce de la Commission pour l'organisa
            tion de notre fête annuelle .
            La danseuse Ida Bianca s'y rendra
            pour répéter sa "Danse flamboyante"
               de Ravin.
Pierre a un geste las, qui exprime le peu d'intérêt qu'il prendra à
cette réunion;mais, tenant à garder la sympathie de son Président, il
dit au chasseur de répondre qu'il se rendra à la réunion. Puis, il rêve de
nouveau à sa chère Marthe ,en considérant sa photo,placée sur son bureau.

5e TABLEAU .- Sous-Titre .- AU CERCLE ROYAL .- La danseuse Ida Bianca est
présentée aux membres de la Commission des Fêtes .—

         La loge de la diva .- Ces Messieurs font cercle autour d'Ida
Pierre arrive, le Directeur du Cercle le présente à la danseuse qui,le
trouvant joli garçon, exerce ses talents de jolie femme et fascine le
jeune homme de son regard . Ida demande qu'on la laisse procéder à sa toilette ,et au moment du départ, Pierre, resté le dernier se retourne et ée
change un dernier regadr avec cellequi a su si bien le séduire dès l'abord
Sitôt parti, Ida a un geste las et dit " Tant pis !" Puis,elle fait venir
sa femme de chambre et procède à sa toilette .

Fig. 4. A sample of a 'B' version of category four scripts: *La Broyeuse de coeurs* (1912).

sit on a pallet'.[5] Version 'B': 'In an attic, three children sit around a table, which with a bed and two chairs make up the sparse furniture of these poor people'.[6] The pallet of the first version becomes, in the 'B' version, a complete décor, with table, bed and chairs. In another instance, what was in the 'A' version described as 'a vision of the mother'[7] changes in the 'B' version to: 'But a vision appears: the children's mother, flanked by an angel, contemplates the orphans and blesses them before disappearing'.[8] Therefore, from one version to another, more than a simple change has occured: the vision of the mother has in fact materialised.

Third category: 'C' versions

Now, we will add to these first two categories of texts without filmstrips, texts accompanied by a filmstrip. The collection of deposited screenplays does in fact comprise manuscripts to which frames of the film were stapled. The filmstrip, stapled to the screenplay, offers undeniable proof that the film was shot. The 'C' versions are then those *screenplays accompanied by a filmstrip, which are in fact summaries of the film, written in prose, as it would have been printed in the catalogue*. Distinguishing them from 'A' and 'B' versions, they bear the designation 'to the copyist'.

Our third category enables us to compare the 'B' version with the 'C' version of the same title. Hence the 'B' version of *Toto gâte-sauce*, (Pathé, 1909, two pages, copyright registration #4252), is labelled 'deposit that conforms to the film' and a 'C' version of *Toto gâte-sauce*, Pathé, 1909, with the seal of the Bibliothèque Nationale, (one page, copyright registration #2222), is labelled 'to the copyist' which presumably means 'for publication'.

The main characteristic of 'C' versions is the fact that each is without a doubt the summary of a film written after its completion. This is the version that is used to describe the film and is what can be found, directly reproduced, in company catalogues such as Pathé's. For instance, *La photographie accusatrice*, (Thanhouser Company, NewRochelle, New York, 1912, one page, copyright registration #2841), has the label 'to the copyist'. We may compare it to the 'B' version of the same title: *La photographie accusatrice*, (Thanhouser Company, NewRochelle, New York, 1912, three pages, copyright registration #4221). This version is labelled 'deposit that conforms to the film'. Whereas the 'C' version is a three-paragraph summary of the action, the 'B' version of the same title is a far more detailed version, and divided into tableaux, describes all those elements relevant to the film's direction, such as the text of the intertitles. The 'C' version, which is, once

FILMS PATHÉ FRÈRES

VENTE & LOCATION : 104, Rue de Paris, VINCENNES

8e Série. - Scènes Dramatiques.   FILMS VALETTA

LA BROYEUSE DE CŒURS

Scène de la vie cruelle par M. de MORLHON

Pierre de Brézeux a tout pour être heureux. Riche, aimable, doué d'une santé de fer, il est fiancé à une jeune fille charmante, qu'il adore, et dont il est profondément aimé. Ce bonheur, hélas ! allait être détruit, par la rencontre d'une femme, d'une sirène, qui devait bouleverser sa vie.

C'est au cours d'une répétition organisée au cercle royal que Pierre, en sa qualité de membre de la commission des fêtes, rencontre, pour la première fois, Ida Bianca, célèbre par sa danse flamboyante. Inquiet de l'émotion étrange qu'il ressent auprès de cette charmeuse, sensation encore accrue par le spectacle de cette femme dansant dans un costume suggestif, révélant des formes impeccables, Pierre, dans une minute de raison, essaie d'échapper à cette fascination. Mais il ne peut résister à l'entraînement de ses sens. Aussi, lorsqu'il reçoit d'Ida un billet de rendez-vous, écrit-il à Marthe, sa fiancée, pour l'avertir qu'une affaire urgente l'empêchera de lui rendre, ce jour-là, sa visite quotidienne. Attablés au Pavillon du Bois, Pierre et Ida devisent joyeusement. Soudain, deux femmes sont devant eux, Marthe et sa mère. Pierre, très pâle, balbutie quelques phrases intelligibles d'excuses. Marthe, indignée, et douloureusement atteinte par la trahison de Pierre, refuse de revoir son fiancé.

Et Pierre qui, dans le secret de son cœur, aime toujours Marthe, devient le jouet de la séduisante Ida. Mordu par la jalousie et définitivement esclavagé, de Brézeux, torturé, voit un toréador, le célèbre Nuovita, s'amouracher d'Ida, et celle-ci se faire un jeu d'affoler cette proie facile — pour mieux s'assurer le cœur de son amant.

Nuovita, dans l'exaltation de sa passion, écrit à Ida que, si elle demeure inflexible, il se fera tuer dans sa lutte contre le taureau. Un bouquet de violettes à son corsage sera le signal d'espoir. Mais Pierre, qui a reçu la lettre en l'absence d'Ida, oublie la missive et cette négligence cause la mort de Nuovita qui, désespéré, se jette au-devant des terribles cornes.

Pierre et Ida, bouleversés par ce drame, comprenant, devant leur crime involontaire, la fragilité de leur passion, se séparent.

L'amour sincère, profond et chaste, a des ressources inépuisables. Marthe ne devait pas tarder à tendre son front, en signe de pardon, à celui qu'elle n'avait pas cessé d'aimer.

Ce drame, interprété avec une grande intensité d'émotion par des artistes éminents, est mis en valeur, tantôt par le décor d'un milieu bien parisien, tantôt par le cadre merveilleux des Pyrénées, ou par le spectacle mouvementé, coloré et sauvage d'une corrida.

Demander les affiches 120 × 160 *et* 240 × 320.

MOT DE CODE **Rencontre**	Longueur 850 mètres Coloris 738 mètres	N° 5787 Virage : 49 fr.

Fig. 5. Catalogue version of *La broyeuse de coeurs*.

again, always accompanied by a filmstrip, is the summary of the screenplay. Moreover, the layout of these versions corresponds to the printing format of the company catalogues. In some instances, a page of the company catalogue was deposited instead of the usual roneotyped document. We explained previously that it was common practice to use certain versions of screenplays as texts in the catalogues for the purpose of describing films. Yet, I also noticed in the course of my research that there did not always exist a 'C' version of a certain title. This suggests that some texts may have been lost, and/or that several registered screenplays were not necessarily shot, a practice that is still common today.

Fourth category: the complete chain

Now that we have identified, qualified and segmented 'A', 'B' and 'C' versions, we may go on to our last category, which represents the completed chain, formed precisely by the sum of all the different versions: The first version without a filmstrip (A), the version without a filmstrip bearing the designation 'deposit that conforms to the film' (B), and lastly the version accompanied by a strip of frames and bearing the mention 'to the copyist' and/or a catalogue page (C). The fourth category then represents deposits that illustrate the complete chain: *An 'A' version that was deposited prior to a 'B' version; a 'B' version that always bears the inscription 'deposit that conforms to the film' and finally the 'C' version, a summary of the film written in prose, as it appears in company catalogues, accompanied by a film-strip.*

As an example of our research, we have reconstituted the complete chain of all the different versions of a particular title, a screenplay written by Mr Camille de Morlhon, called *La Broyeuse de coeurs* (Pathé, 1912). We recovered the first version (A) at the Cinémathèque française (manuscript #3705). It is a manuscript in two parts, of fourteen and thirteen pages respectively. This first version of the text is divided into tableaux and contains intertitles, as well as technical information. The following is an example:

> He almost stops his gesture, but still hands the coat over to the groom. Pierre tries to struggle, haphazardly invoking some pretext, but the president counters him with subtle manoeuvres. He cannot find the strength to overcome them, since he has difficulty mastering himself ...[10]

We then have this underlined note:

> Either in the subtitle of no. 6, or in the letter of no. 4, we will indicate that this is a rehearsal in costume, for orchestra only, not for the

dance. The end of 6 and the beginning of 8, the dance rehearsal, will be of the shortest possible footage. (p.5)[11]

The 'B' version is kept at the Bibliothèque de l'Arsenal. It is a screenplay without a filmstrip, which bears the notice 'conforms to film', (copyright registration #5537). A seven-page work in two parts, it is divided into 52 tableaux, with intertitles. This particular version is shorter than the one held by the Cinémathèque Française and clearly indicates the use of intertitles, projected handwritten letters and set changes. It is a 'B' version in which the 'deposit conforms to the film'. Finally, the last link of this chain is the film's summary, written after completion, with an accompanying filmstrip, the 'C' version: *La Broyeuse de coeurs*, by Mr Camille de Morlhon, Pathé, 1912, summary of the film, catalogue page, copyright registration #972, labelled 'to the copyist'. We were also able to find the version printed in the catalogue, which corresponds to the 'C' version registered at the Bibliothèque Nationale.

Therefore, it is quite clear that the texts written in prose in the form of summaries and registered with accompanying frames are texts written after the completion of the actual film. It is certain that these titles were made as films. Moreover, the texts registered without accompanying frames and without the mention 'dépôt conforme à la vue' are the very first versions of a screenplay ('A' versions). It should be noted that, as stated by Valéria Ciezar and Agnès Margraff of the Gaumont production of 1908–09 and of Pathé's of 1913: 'We still do not have a clear idea of the proportion of screenplays that were actually shot' and 'it seems several titles were never shot'. In fact, Margraff goes on to state that of 511 registered screenplays, only 242 films (less than half) could be traced and verified as actually having been shot.[12]

Since 1985, I have checked the correlation and links between different registration numbers associated with a single title. Sure enough, on a sample of no less than 300 titles, three times out of five, we were able to find only 'A' versions (for example, *La photographie révélatrice*), versions without frames and without the inscription 'dépôt conforme à la vue'. As we have stated earlier, these are the initial screenplays which were written prior to shooting. If the registration protocol of texts with filmstrips or those labelled 'deposit that conforms to the film' is honored, we can say the 'A' versions are very much screenplays in the contemporary definition of the term: a text divided into scenes, tableaux or shots, which puts forth a description of the action to be shot, and which is written before the shooting starts.

Finally, the 'B' versions or 'deposits that conform to the film', are intermediate versions and they clearly make reference to the film. Nowadays this is called the shooting script, the version closest to the film. In the future, by accessing the computerised records of the Bibliothèque de l'Arsenal, we will be able to

```
    IV.- L'ATRE DE DIVERSES CHEMINEES DIFFERENTES DE STYLE ET
DE MODELE.

        1ère cheminée.- Une petite fille se tient devant la che-
-minée où sont déposés ses souliers. Elle est en longue chemise
de nuit . Tout a coup , par la cheminée, elle reçoit: Une panoplie
de soldat . Pleurs.

        2e cheminée.- Le petit garçon (même jeu) reçoit des fers
à repasser : Pleurs

        3e cheminée. La demi-mondaine (même jeu) un lapin vivant

    4e      "      Le vieux beau      "    "  un martinet

    5e      "      La vieille dame    "    "  une pipe

    6e      "      Le noble duc       "    "  un clysopompe

    7e cheminée  Le cul de jatte   (même jeu) Un pantalon (ce-
                                                -lui-ci a mis sa
                                                casquette dans la
                                                cheminée )

    8e      "      La cuisinière     "    "  Un roman de
                                                Pierre Loti
```

Fig. 6. The screenplay provides a blueprint for editing: the script for scene four of *Le bonhomme Noël* (1907).

assemble exhaustive lists of the actual number of screenplays which were never shot. Nonetheless, at this time we can assert that the texts deposited at the Bibliothèque Nationale by Gaumont and Pathé are not all summaries written after the completion of the films.

The status of the texts having been concretely substanciated, we may now go on to the last section of our study and analyse the screenplays as texts describing films to be shot: 'A' versions, screenplays without the accompanying filmstrips. We have already seen a few examples of these.

Analysis

Far from being vague, general or theatrical, the first screenplays show a definite sensitivity and knowledge of the potential of film language, and its developments can be traced and witnessed in the written texts. Before we start, let's read the following excerpt of a screenplay titled *Le petit béquillard* and

try to imagine how this film could look by visualising the images the text conveys as it unfolds:

Le petit béquillard, Pathé 1907, four pages …
Tableau #2
In the street. The prowlers are stationed in front of the cabaret entrance door and keep a lookout. Nobody comes. They climb up to the window of the first floor, break open a shutter and enter.
Tableau #3
The bedroom. We see them come in through the window. They pounce on the female cabaret-keeper and one of them stabs her. Short struggle. The little boy wakes up in his bed, sees everything, and they gag him. A dog enters the room and barks loudly, the men grab him, open the window and throw him out.[13]

Early cinema screenplays remind us of the films and conjure up images of other films which were never shot or have been lost, and they still clearly evoke the particular style and motley aesthetic of the films made before 1914. This exercise in visualisation – which calls attention to the work of the screenwriter – having been completed, let us now examine how the screenplay determines and designs the film's editing strategy; how it structures space and time (whether or not it is linear); how it constructs a narrative point of view; and how it influences storytelling style. Indeed, a good number of cinematic practices basic to what we now refer to as filmic language clearly reveal themselves as present in these earlier texts.

It is worth noting the manner in which the texts attempt, within the screenwriting conventions and norms already in place by that time, to describe exactly what the spectator should see and understand, instead of simply 'telling a story' and/or of explaining a character's thoughts, as in a novel. Thus the texts describe the movements or gestures that express the idea that is to be felt and perceived by the spectator. Even in 1907, they don't fall into the beginner screenwriter's trap which is to write what one character is thinking instead of showing the character in action. For example, in *Le perroquet de Mme Ducordon* (Pathé, 1907): 'All of a sudden, he raises a hand to his forehead: he has an idea'. [14] *Une partie de cartes interrompue* (Pathé, 1907) further illustrates this point: 'Our three players sit around the table and one of them gestures suddenly that he has an idea. He asks for a pen and paper and writes a letter (...)'. [15] The screenplay describes what will unfold and in doing so describes the way the action will be seen and heard. In *Le petit béquillard*, the screenplay even foresees showing the source of a sound: 'A dog enters and barks loudly, the men grab him, open the window and throw him out. [16] The story is told by accumulation of actions and situations; the screenplay does not explain, it sets down what will be shown. For example, in *Le bonhomme Noël*, (Gaumont, 1907, four pages):

Scene 1 – HEAVEN'S GATE – A fenced wall in which there is a door. At the right of the door is a look-out. In front of the turret there is a folding bed and a table. On the door, a sign reads: 'Heaven' translated into several languages. In the foreground, clouds roll by, blocking part of the view. [17]

As well, these scripts sometimes correct and re-adjust the unfolding of the action. In *La policière* (Pathé, 1907, four pages, copyright registration #3903) a tableau is crossed out, thus modifying the action:

Tableau 17 (crossed out)
Under the archways. The police commissioner arrives with his men and they follow Lisa.
Tableau 17: Under the archways. Lisa enters and singles out three people. The police commissioner steps in, pointing his gun. The officers arrest everyone. [18]

If the works of André Gaudreault and Tom Gunning have convincingly described the non-continuous style and monstrative system of pre-1914 films, it has to be pointed out that early cinema screenplays shed an albeit discrete but essential light on the way the découpage developed and was planned in writing. The thought process involved in telling a story with a montage of segments was already present as early as 1907. These remaining texts – which are much more numerous than the films – force us to re-examine the use of continuity and non-continuity features in early cinema storytelling.

From 1907 on, the screenplays are riddled with parallel editing configurations as in *Pauvres gosses*, Pathé, 1907, #2740 (a rendering of the story of Tom Thumb) where the tableaux alternate as they describe simultaneous actions: the mother at home, the children out in the woods and the father at work.

Continuity is not only given priority: it is a well-mastered screenwriting technique, quite the opposite of what prevailed in the very first years of the cinema. Were the films themselves less continuous than the scripts? Could it be that the films became non-continuous through multiple showings and the degradation of the film itself, or were they intrinsically monstrative?

We can see this preoccupation with continuity in *L'acrobate*, Gaumont, 1907, one page [recto-verso], copyright registration #3390:

4. ... Goes to the neighbour's.
5. Working class interior ... The woman goes to the theatre to warn the clown.
6. Inside a circus. The clown goes near her.
7. Passageway or green-room inside the

circus. The woman tells him the child is very ill.[19]

In *Le bonhomme Noël*, (Gaumont, 1907, four pages), note the accelerated découpage between each tableau. The preoccupation with montage is quite evident. The manner in which the screenplay goes about cutting the action in order to go from one chimney to another is also worth noting:

1st chimney – A little girl stands close to a chimney where her shoes lie. She is wearing a long nightshirt. All of a sudden, a suit of armour comes down the chimney. Tears.

2nd chimney – A little boy (same action) receives smoothing-irons: tears.

3rd chimney – A demimondaine (same action) a live rabbit.

4th chimney – handsome old man (same action) a whip.

5th chimney – An old lady (same action) a pipe. [etc.][20]

Some screenplays also contain flashbacks, as in *Partie de cartes interrompue*, Pathé, 1907 #1730:

... 2 days later. The shopwindow of a cabaret. Our three players are playing, suddenly the friend appears, he has two black eyes, they invite him to the game, but he remembers the beating he took, he refuses and leaves (First shot: the player gesturing his refusal).[21]

Finally, it was not surprising to find many circular narratives where the last shot is identified in the script as being the same as the first tableau (*Pauvres gosses*, #2740), restoring the initial order. This circularity of the written story is important to note because many historians thought that the exhibitors took the liberty of showing the end shot at the beginning. Reading the screenplays teaches us that this practice was planned in the writing stage. Also found, were quite a few chase films (that it's an understatement), such as *Le pharmacien distrait*, Pathé 1907, #1415:

5th tableau: In front of the drugstore. The maid gets in her car and drives off. The busy pharmacist steps out and rushes after the car.

6th tableau: In front a café terrace. The car goes by. The pharmacist pursues it ...

7th tableau: The car goes by followed by the pharmacist on his bicycle. He runs into a window-glass maker. The window-glass maker joins in the chase.

8th tableau: A street corner. The car goes by, followed by the pharmacist and his pursuers ...[22]

The analysis of the developments of film language as described in the screenplays is only partial here and has been pursued elsewhere (see note 17). This completes, for now, our two-part study of French early cinema screenplays, the first being mainly descriptive and the second analytical.

We have seen what distinguishes screenplay versions written before film production from versions written after production. Needless to say, multiple versions of a single title are an important source of study for researchers.

Moreover, if the period of 'the cinema of attractions' demonstrated preoccupations with continuity of content but of non-continuity in terms of the filmic discourse, the screenplays of the 1907–14 epoch offer proof of the passage toward narration, by way of continuity of content as well as of the filmic discourse, achieved through written découpage and montage patterns. As of 1907 and certainly before that, the screenplays create a continuous style with the use of the cut on action. From one tableau to the next, these cuts create the continuity of the narrative and of the actions on all levels: visual, spatial, temporal and semantic. Lastly, we have shown the richness and the diversity of a corpus of screenplays, which we are still exploring.

May we dream of the day a screenplay will find its forgotten film? We look forward to the day when we will discuss screenplays with the same complicity and passion we do films, a day when several scholars will have the opportunity to read the same screenplays, each developing his or her own line of thought. It is this kind of diversity around a common group of texts that leads to progress in research on the role of early scenarios.

Acknowledgements

Translated from French by Isabelle Raynauld and Daniel

Cholette; reprinted, with the kind permission of Michel Marie and the University of the Sorbonne Press, from *Les vingt premières années du cinéma français*, eds. Jean Gili, Michele Lagny, Michel Marie and Vincent Pinel (Paris: Presses de la Sorbonne Nouvelle, 1995).

I want to thank Daniel Cholette, a graduate student in Film Studies at the University of Montreal, for his help in translating this article. ♠

Notes

1.   A state of affairs rendered evident at the international conference «Le scénario», on the screenplay, organised by the Quebec Association of Film Studies (Association québécoise des études cinématographiques) held in Montreal at the Musée des Beaux Arts in 1992; more than 30 lecturers discussed the screenplay from theoretical, historical and analytical standpoints. See also *Creative Screenwriting*, published in Washington.

2.   Raynauld, Isabelle, Le scénario de film comme texte; histoire, théorie et lecture (s) du scénario. De Georges Méliès à Marguerite Duras et Jean-Luc Godard, PhD dissertation, Université de Paris VII, 1990, 356 pages.

3.   'Les scénarios de la Passion selon Pathé (1902–1914)' in *Une invention du diable? Cinéma des premiers temps et religion*. Published under the direction of R. Cosandey, A. Gaudreault, T. Gunning (Sainte-Foy, Lausanne, Presses de l'Université Laval, Editions Payot, 1992), 131–141.

4.   In the original French: 'dépôt conforme à la vue'.

5.   In the French text: 'Dans une mandsarde, trois enfants sont assis sur un grabat'.

6.   The original text reads: 'Dans une mansarde, trois enfants sont assis à une table, qui avec le lit et deux chaises forment l'unique mobilier des pauvres gens'.

7.   In French: 'vision de la mère'.

8.   'Mais une vision apparaît: la mère des enfants avec un ange contemplent les orphelins et les bénit, puis disparaît'.

9.   In French: 'au multicopiste'.

10.   In the original text: 'Il empêche presque de force le geste d'être achevé, redonne le manteau au groom. Pierre tente bien de lutter, invoquant un prétexte au hasard, mais le président lui fait une douce violence, qu'il n'a pas le courage de surmonter, ayant toutes les peines du monde à se vaincre lui-même ...'

11.   In French: 'N.B. Soit dans le sous-titre du no 6, soit

dans la lettre du no 4, on n'indiquera qu'il ne s'agit là que d'une répétition en costume, et uniquement pour l'orchestre et non pas pour la danse. La fin du 6 et le commencement du 8, C.A.D. la partie de l'esquisse des pas, seront d'ailleurs d'un métrage le plus court possible' (5).

12.   Valéria Ciezar, Les scénarios Gaumont (1908–09): Première approche thématique. MA. dissertation, under the direction of Michèle Magny and Marc Vernet, Université de Paris III, Sorbonne Nouvelle, 1993, (p.9). In French: 'On est sans certitude quant à la proportion de scénarios effectivement tournés' Agnès Margraff, Les scénarios Pathé de l'année 1913. MA. dissertation under the direction of Michèle Magny, Université de Paris III, Sorbonne Nouvelle, 1993, 69. In French: 'de nombreux titres semblent n'avoir jamais été tournés'.

13.   Le petit béquillard, Pathé, 1907, four pages ... 2e tableau: Dans la rue. Les rôdeurs sont devant la porte du cabaret ils font le guet. Personne ne vient. Ils escaladent la fenêtre du premier, font sauter un volet de fermeture et pénètrent à l'intérieur. 3e tableau: Chambre à coucher. On les voit entrer après avoir ouvert la fenêtre. Ils se jettent sur la carabetière, un surtout plus acharné la poignarde. Courte lutte. Le petit dans son lit se réveille, voit la scène, ils le bâillonnent. Un chien fait irruption aboie avec force, les hommes le prennent, ouvrent le judas et le jettent au travers.

14.   In French: 'Tout à coup, il se frappe le front: il a une idée'.

15.   'Nos trois joueurs sont attablés, soudain l'un d'eux fait signe qu'il a une idée, il demande de quoi écrire, rédige une lettre ...'

16.   'Un chien fait irruption aboie avec force, les hommes le prennent, ouvrent le judas et le jettent au travers'. On the topic of sound, see also: Colloque International organisé pour Domitor (association internationale), la Cinémathèque Française et l'Université Paris III: *Pathé Fréres 1900–1914*, conférencière, «Importance, présence et représentation du son dans les scénarios et les films Pathé dits muets», décembre 1996, Paris, France. (to be published). Colloque de Cerisy-La-Salle, conférencière, «Scénarios et films de Georges Méliès: approches narratives», *Georges Méliès et le deuxiéme siècle du cinéma*, août 1996, Cerisy, France (to be published). Colloque International de Domitor, Cinema Turns 100, conférencière, «Pratiques scénaristiques en France et aux États-Unis avant1914. Informations visuelles et sonores», juin 1994 (Museum of Modern Art/New York University, New York).

17.   The original text reads: 'SCÈNE 1 - LA PORTE DU

CIEL. - Un mur de cloture dans lequel s'ouvre une porte. A droite de la porte une guérite. Devant la guérite un pliant et une petite table. Sur la porte un écriteau: 'Ciel' en plusieurs langues. Au premier plan, des nuages qui marchent, limitant le champ en avant.'

18. The original French text reads: 'Tableau 17 (raturé) Sous les voutes. Le commissaire arrive avec les agents, ils suivent Lisa.
Tableau 17: Sous les voutes. Lisa entre et désigne les trois personnes. Le commissaire s'avance le révolver au poing. Les agents emballent tout le monde.

19. The original French reads:
4. ... Va chez une voisine.
5. Intérieur d'ouvriers ... La femme va prévenir le clown au théâtre.
6. Intérieur du cirque. Le clown ... se rend près d'elle.
7. Couloir du cirque ou foyer. La femme lui explique que l'enfant est au plus mal.

20. 1re cheminée – Une petite fille se tient devant une cheminée où sont déposés ses souliers. Elle est en longue chemise de nuit. Tout à coup, par la cheminée, elle reHoit: une panoplie de soldats. Pleurs.
2e cheminée – Le petit garçon (même jeu) reçoit des fers à repasser: pleurs.
3e cheminée – La demi-mondaine (même jeu) un lapin vivant.
4e cheminée – Le vieux beau (même jeu) un martinet.
5e cheminée – La vieille dame (même jeu) une pipe. [etc.]

21. 2 jours après – La devanture d'un cabaret. Nos trois joueurs sont en train de jouer, à ce moment parait leur camarade, les deux yeux pochés, ils l'invitent à prendre part aux jeu, mais celui-ci qui se souvient de la correction qu'il a reçue refuse énergiquement et s'éloigne (Premier plan: le joueur faisant un geste de refus). #1730.

22. 5e tableau. Devant la pharmacie. La bonne remonte en voiture et s'éloigne. Le pharmacien sort affairé et se précipite dans la direction de la voiture.
6e tableau. Devant une terrasse de café. La voiture passe. Le pharmacien la poursuit ...
7e tableau. Une rue. La voiture passe poursuivie par le pharmacien en bicyclette, il renverse un vitrier et abandonnant la machine il continue sa course. Le vitrier se joint aux poursuivants.
8e tableau. Un coin de rue. La voiture passe suivie du pharmacien et de ses poursuivants ...

Film History, Volume 9, pp. 269–276, 1997. Copyright © John Libbey & Company
ISSN: 0892-2160. Printed in Australia

A screenwriting sampler from the Moving Picture World

The following three articles, which originally appeared in the *Moving Picture World*, give a sense of the trade discourse on screenwriting in the 1910s.

Epes Winthrop Sargent, whose contribution to the profession is discussed at length in Edward Azlant's essay, wrote about vaudeville and motion pictures for *Variety*, the *Moving Picture World* and other publications. He was also a story editor for the Lubin Manufacturing Co. The article reprinted here constitutes an early history of screenwriting from 1894 to 1914.

Jeanie Macpherson, a former actress at Biograph, directed films for Universal in the early 1910s. In 1915, she went to work for Cecil B. DeMille for whom she wrote screenplays such as

The Heart of Nora Flynn (1916), *Joan the Woman* (1917), *Old Wives for New* (1918), *Male and Female* (1919), *Manslaughter* (1922), *The King of Kings* (1927) and *Madame Satan* (1930).

Lloyd Lonergan was the brother-in-law of Edwin Thanhouser, founder of the Thanhouser Film Corporation of New Rochelle, New York. As story editor and chief scenarist for Thanhouser, Lonergan co-authored the script for the company's first serial, *The Million Dollar Mystery* (1914–15). He also wrote *Robin Hood* (1913), *The Price of Her Silence* (1915), *Her Beloved Enemy* (1917), and other films. His brother, Philip, was also a screenwriter and wrote adaptations of *The Mill and the Floss* (1915), *King Lear* (1916), *Silas Marner* (1916) and other stories.

The literary side of pictures

Epes Winthrop Sargent

Suppose, before we get too deep into the subject, that you take a look at the forgotten side of what this title implies. Now and then one of our cherished goats wanders from its own fireside at the call of someone who says that pictures are not literature, but we call it back, because we're careful of our goats and don't let them associate with such persons.

Stop a minute and think. Literature is old, centuries old. It started 'way back; possibly before the flood. It ought to be good by this time if, like wine and cheese, it gets savor from age. Photoplay writ-

ing is no bearded veteran. Photoplay writing was born some time or another in 1909. Can you ask the six-year-old to have the erudition of the ages?

Now to beat out the possible (and probable) objector, we'll revise that statement, but with mental reservations. The photoplay writing game started somewhere between 1894 and 1896. Don't ask just precisely when. If we could tell we would not be writing this stuff. We would be over in the Treasury Department or some place in Washington, making out next year's corn crop reports. We never said we were *that* good.

But it was about 1898 that the first editor was employed. Then there were three companies over here that lasted overnight. One of them was the Biograph. They had been doing the Jefferson family until we were sick of them. The Jeffersons were big in the Biograph in those days and if you saw a fisherman who hooked himself in the seat of his panties it was C.B. Jefferson, or Joe, Jr. or someone of the Jefferson family who were more numerous in those days than Eddie Foy's family is at present. Every time we asked Austin Fynes who a new Biograph player was he found out and added a new Jefferson to the already numerous family.

About this time Roy McCardell was off the New York *World*. In those days McCardell spent about two-thirds of his time with the paper of that title and about one-third holding out for more money, because he was making good. This was one of his off moments and he was 'writing pictures' for the then *Standard*. They were not moving pictures in the sense now employed, though they were indeed moving. McCardell used to write about ten captions telling a more or less complete story. Then he and the boss would hire a lot of models – mostly girls – and go out and make pictures for the captions. Somebody on the Biograph must have read the *Standard*, for presently McCardell was hired to go down to Thirteenth street and Broadway and write pictures for the Biograph. To be exact it was for the Mutoscope, then a nickel in the slot machine. They didn't think much of the projection machine in those days. It was all mutoscope.

Anyhow, Roy wrote the stuff and he was the first man on either side of the water to be hired for no other purpose than to write pictures. He did the work very successfully until he got the idea for Mr and Mrs Nagg, the first cousins to the present Jarr family, and he went the rest of the way down to the place with the gilded dome, but he has kept on writing pictures to this day and he is still one of the most successful farcical writers. In passing, the New York *World* later gave two other writers to the business. With the formation of the Thanhouser Company, Lloyd Lonergan, a brother-in-law of the founder of the company, was induced to leave the paper and write stories for the films. Until the growth of the Thanhouser concern made it necessary for

him to concentrate on the big stuff like 'The Million Dollar Mystery', he did most of the stories for Thanhouser and later for the Princess, as well. Considering the number of stories produced in proportion to the percentage of hits, we incline to the belief that Mr Lonergan has a better batting average than any man in the game today.

The third member of the New York *World* trio is Russell E. Smith, who recently quit that paper to become connected with the Mutual.

But this brings us too close to the moment. Let's back up to the old days. At the start the people about the studio suggested the stories done, and some of them should have been electrocuted. Now and then some bold spirit would send an idea to the company – any company – and sometimes the company 'took pleasure' in paying $5 or $10 for the idea. Even those prices were liberal for the goods delivered. The pictures crept up from the old fifty-foot lengths in a single scene to several hundred feet, but it was the Edison Company that stayed the ebbing tide and brought it back to flood with *The Great Train Robbery*.

Presently most of the 'then' companies had photoplay editors. Rollin S. Sturgeon was the Vitagraph editor, replacing J. Stuart Blackton and Albert E. Smith, who had previously done the work. If Archer McMackin was not the first Essanay editor, his predecessor did not make noise enough to be heard in New York. It was Essanay, we *think*, who first advertised in the *Editor*, a paper devoted to the authors, for scripts, and for many years the 'we pay from $10 to $100', and 'no literary experience required' were the standard arguments. The latter was more truthful than the first. The $10 was closer to the mark than the hundred, but literary skill was not required. Any right-minded editor would have taken any half-way idea and have fixed it up. We think it was Sturgeon who first offered a sheet of suggestions. The idea was generally accepted. Essanay had almost a small booklet and Lubin had a mimeograph sheet, later replaced by a printed sheet which we wrote. We were the third editor, taking over the Lubin scripts in August 1909.

Those were the happy days. If you get enough idea from a script to suggest a play, you wrote it out and coaxed some director to take it. Most always he did, if the idea was good and he liked that sort of idea. There were no trained writers in those days

ROY L. McCARDELL   BANNISTER MERWIN   RICHARD HARDING DAVIS   HAROLD MacGRATH

EPES WINTHROP SARGENT   EMMET CAMPBELL HALL   J. BERG ESENWEIN   MARC EDMUND JONES

A Group of Photo-playwrights

Fig. 1. 'A Group of Photo-playwrights' as seen in Robert Grau's *The Theatre of Science* (1914; reprint Benjamin Blom 1969), 27.

– and few good ones. We remember the morning we almost fell down those flights or stairs to show the boss Emmett Campbell Hall's 'Indian Blood', the first of the now numerous 'reversion to type' stories. There was a long argument as to whether or not he would be glad to get $25 or whether $35 would not stir him to better efforts. The $35 won, but later on Hall got $5 for a script from Selig and a few scenes on a burning bridge cost about sixty times what the script brought. Later Selig was one of Hall's best markets and only his fear of the big cities kept him from being the Selig editor. Before that Biograph had offered him a chance as staff writer, but Hall had a home in Glen Echo, near Washington, and he would not be coaxed. Lawrence McCloskey did coax him on to the Lubin staff last fall, but the last we heard Hall had gone back to the beautiful country. But this again gets ahead of the story. But before we back up, Hall's 'His Trust' and 'His Trust Fulfilled', done by Biograph, was the first two-part story not derived from some book. There had been multiples, released in series, before then, but the

closest approach to an original was Vitagraph's presentation of the Rev. Madison Peters' very free adaptation of the story of Moses, in five parts, which was released one part weekly.

Another Washingtonian, Capt. Charles Kiener, of the Copyright office, had begun to attract attention. Like Hall he wrote a full, but practical working script. He did a lot of business with Lubin for a time, but went to Kalem, as a contract writer, and has but very recently reappeared as a free lance. His best work has been some historicals on the early California days, but he has also done some excellent melodramas.

It is not very generally known that Bannister Merwin was one of the early birds, but he submitted one story in 1909. It was a capital story, but he wanted $100 for it and he was making that and more for his fiction. After a couple of attempts he dropped out until Ashley Miller, of Edison, got him back in the game. For a couple of years he was the Edison star, but last November he changed over to the London Film Company.

Pop Hoadley was another of the early birds. As C.B. Hoadley, he had pushed his newspaper success to the point where he had to quit, and he bought a fruit farm. In the interval of packing apples he wrote stuff and early turned his attention to plays. In time he was brought East to become successor in the Imp to Giles R. Warren, who went to Lubin along with Miss Florence Lawrence and Arthur Johnson. Since then he has been editor for Champion, Great Northern, Powers and Imp. Until recently he was the editor for the Biograph-Klaw and Erlanger combination. Like so many others, he sold his first story to Lubin. He is now a free lance.

William H. Kitchell, then known as 'the literary carpenter', was one of the early contributors and still has to see his first story on the screen, 'The Stamp of Labor'. It was a good story but it meant a big production at a time when big productions were not in favor. Edmund S. Hirsch, of Brooklyn, is another whose first story is still in the Lubin films, a story of Betsy Ross that was bought because it could be made in the actual locations, but never was made because it needed better actors than Lubin had in those days. Since then, Benjamin Barondess and Edward J. Montague have risen to contest the Brooklyn championship, but Hirsch was the first, outside of the Vitagraph string.

Frank E. 'Spec' Woods was then the motion picture editor of the *Dramatic Mirror*, and on the side he gave Biograph comedies, including the 'Jones' series, which first brought to the front the late John Cumpson and Miss Mary Pickford, though Miss Pickford's most marked success was 'All on Account of the Milk', which was written by Mrs Laurie Mackin, who still appears in pictures. Mr Woods is notable as being the one commentator on [the] photoplay who never wrote a book on how to do it.

On the other hand William Lord Wright was first in the field with a book (even if it said nothing about leaders), and his second book has just come from the press. He is a newspaper editor in Bellefontaine, Ohio, and writes in his spare time, though no one knows what a country editor's spare time is. There must be *some* spare time, though, for he contributes a page or more a week to the *Dramatic Mirror* and is known as the 'sure fire' writer of advertising plays about the meanest job a man can make good with.

Another book author is Arthur Leeds, who used to be a star Selig and Essanay writer. He was once an actor and lecturer, turning to pictures. He is now editor of *The Photoplay Author* and head of the photoplay section of the Home Correspondence Schools. He is doing very little original work at present.

Another is A.W. Thomas, of the *Photoplay Magazine* and the *Scenario Writer*. He has done a few plays but nothing to attract marked attention. He holds pretty closely to the editorial end.

A lot of the old timers have dropped from view. Charles Simms is never heard of and Charles Jenkins is editing a sheet in the Canadian Rockies. Mrs Elizabeth de Binde Yorke, who used to be a Biograph star, seems to have quit. Some of the others seem to have dropped so far from sight that they are not even remembered.

On the other hand take H. Tipton Steck. He used to be glad to take $15 for half reel stuff. Now he is manager of production for Essanay. Sturgeon is another of the 'firsts' who is still well to the fore and our own Louis Reeves Harrison came early and stayed on. He was one of the early Biographers and Vitagraphers. He was here ahead of his day, for he is a man with a literary past as honorable as his present or his future; indeed, in the early days, he had to wait for the business to grow up to his standard. It is one of the signs of the times that it did.

Another whom Biograph started was George Hennessey. He was foxy in his early days. They would not believe that he could write dramas. They were in the market for comedies. He wrote comedies until they liked his dramas and for a long time he was the star writer. He is freelancing now, out in Los Angeles. He had written some of the best stories the Biograph ever produced, but you would not think it to look at him quickly. Look twice and you see the brains beneath the apparently listless exterior.

Edwin S. Porter, now of the Famous Players, is another of the 'forty-niners' of the game, and Miss Gene Gauntier has written as many one-reel dramas as any writer living. She will go down in history as the author, adapter or what you will of 'From the Manger to the Cross', but she is far more important than any one story.

But while there were others of those early days, it is not practicable to list them all in separate paragraphs. Mention of Miss Gauntier, very first of the women writers, brings us to others who have made good. Mrs Beta Breuil, or Mrs Hartmann Breuil, was a Vitagraph editor and still a prominent freelance. Mrs Catherine Carr, now of the North American, is another Vita graduate, as is Miss Peggy O'Neill, of the same company. Mrs Louella Parsons, of Essanay, has written little, but many promising writers owe much to her helpful advice.

Miss Hetty Gray Baker gave up a job as a law librarian to become editor for Jack London (Bosworth, Inc.), which is not altogether photoplay's gain, for, in spite of the excellence of her adaptations of this most difficult author, she did better original work, having the imagination of a real creator. Miss Cora Drew has lately come to the fore as a woman writer. Mrs Lillian Sweetser, of Maine, is another and Mrs Betty Fitzgerald, of Gasden, Ala., has the distinction of having won the top price for a regular script from Griffith, of the Reliance, solely for the excellence of her work. Mrs Marguerite Bertsch, the present editor of the Biograph, is a woman writer whose stories show keen insight into affairs, and Miss Maibelle Heikes Justice, a novelist and short story writer, is one of the Selig stars. Her work is exceptional in many ways. Lois Weber (Mrs Phillips Smalley) is another prolific writer of strength and versatility.

Miss Mary Fuller has written some of the smartest stories in which she has appeared, but if we started to list the Edison players who are also writers, we would have to give the complete roster.

George Terwilliger, like 'Spec', came to us from the *Mirror*. He had done some capital work with the Reliance. He is now with Lubin as director and writer. He does mostly two-reel stories. Romaine Fielding is also a Lubin author–director. Shannon Fife, of the same company, took to photoplay because the studio was in the same town with the University of Pennsylvania, in which he was a student. Harry Chandlee, lately added to the list, was a Washington correspondent for a string of small papers. Clay M. Greene is a well-known dramatic author and former Shepherd of the Lambs. McCloskey himself, the head of the brainiest lot of staff writers in the photoplay business, was a Philadelphia newspaper man. Following this writer and Giles Warren, he was the first to put the staff on a business basis, and his organisation is probably the strongest to be found.

The Universal staff is headed by Captain Leslie T. Peacocke, in the East. Captain Peacocke is also a dramatist and novelist. Walter MacNamara was once a member of the staff, as was Pop Hoadley, to say nothing of Hal Reid, who bought more stories for $10 cash each than any man alive or dead. Monte Katterjohn was its most recent head, but he lately went away and is free lancing again, as well as writing most of the moving picture stuff for the Red, Green and Blue Books, otherwise known as the Chromatic circuit.

Two ministers have found success in photoplay, the Rev. E.B. Stockton and the Rev. Sydney S. Booth. Dr Stockton ranges from farce to tragedy, but Mr Booth is at his best in comedy, if he is an Englishman. Perhaps the best paid writer of today is James Oliver Curwood, who does most of his stuff for the Selig Company. He gets the top price and is one of the very, very few novelists who can write a practical photoplay script. Gilson Willetts, who used to be a wholesale dealer in magazine stories, is another Selig star. Harold MacGrath is not a photoplay writer, nor are most of the others whose names appear on the screen as authors, though Jack London is said to be studying the work. James Oppenheim is a real photoplay writer, but the late Thomas W. Hanshew and Richard Harding Davis, Rex Beach and others do their work by proxy.

Others of the new school are Marc Edmund Jones, who came out of a railroad office; John William Kellette, who knows all about linotypes; Harry O. Hoyt, a civil engineer, now managing a theatre in Minneapolis; E.W. Matlack, train dispatcher of the Pennsylvania at Pittsburgh; Guy T. Evans and Frank Clarke, of the same place; Frank K. Shaw, for years on the bench in Maine; Edwin Ray Coffin, a ranchman; Miss Marian Lee Patterson, a magazine writer; Julian Louis Lamothe, of New Orleans; Frank Griffin, formerly of Universal and now with Lubin, and scores of others to whom we offer our apologies in advance.

Among the writing editors are Bennie Schulberg, of the Famous Players; James Dayton, the star of Western Universal; Richard V. Spencer, of K. B.; Richard Willis, Willis Robards, Charles M. Seay, Herbert Brenon, of Imp, and others to whom we also apologise.

Credit for the Series stories would seem to go to Edison, whose manager of negative production, Horace G. Plimpton, was the first to popularise the idea (not forgetting, of course, the Jones series already mentioned), and to Mr Plimpton's ability to get his directors to give the spirit of the author's work, is largely due to the popularity of the book story, though Col. Selig is perhaps the largest buyer of book rights at present.

It has been a big jump from the $10 to $20 of 1909 to the $50 to $100 of today, but the changes to come will be still more marked and it is reasonable to suppose that the story of a few years hence will make these prices seem absurd. Already $1000 and even more has been paid for book rights without the advantage of simultaneous publication in the newspapers, and it is only reasonable to suppose that in the time to come, when the best

of the book rights shall have been exhausted, the author who writes photoplays for photoplay production will command a better price than the man who writes books that may be adapted. John Singer Sargent is the foremost portrait painter of today, but some of his water colors are jokes. The man who works in his proper medium is the man who eventually will command the best prices and we are still not quite up to the real literature of the photoplay.

P.S. And to make the record complete, E.W. Sargent, a former musical and dramatic critic, editor and writer of photoplays, has done several hundred stories for Lubin, two for Imp, two for Vitagraph and seven for Edison. Also about half a mile of photoplay advice and several miles of short stories and novelettes.

Originally published in the *Moving Picture World*, 11 July 1914.

Development of photodramatic writing

Jeanie Macpherson

Writing for the photodrama is becoming more and more difficult every day. Every day new photo-dramatic symbols are being created to take the place of involved action or explanatory subtitles [sic]. As the art progresses, so does the public's understanding of the art, and the methods we used two years ago to explain certain things are now archaic, as, for example, not so long ago, when we wanted to show a man thinking of his sweet-heart, we had him sitting with his head in his hands, casually gazing into a fire, but faded in a vision of his sweet-heart on the scene over his head. Now we get the effect by simply having him bring out her handkerchief, a glove or something which shows the same thing. The audience understands it, and the obvious symbols are no longer a necessity.

Illustrating sub-titles by means of moving pictures is also passed. No longer do we have to describe a scene of a sub-title and then act out the scene. Now a sub-title is being dropped wherever possible and everything told in terms of action. If a woman is going down town to buy a new hat because her old one's worn out, we no longer have to have our actors make a lot of gestures and use two

or three spoken titles. It is simply necessary for them to show the worn, torn ribbon of the hat, with, of course, the necessary expression to show what is to be conveyed. To show a telephone conversation it is no longer necessary to show both parties hanging up the 'phone. If one hangs up the 'phone we know the conversation is discontinued. We no longer have to show a letter inserted more than once or twice. When the audience reads the letter they know that it is in the person's possession and they can follow it. It isn't necessary to show it from time to time.

We have found out it isn't necessary for a photodrama to have only one dramatic scene, but each scene must be a drama in itself. The whole picture must be made up of a series of small dramas. This makes the completed drama a mosaic of little ones. Scenes that have no dramatic value in them, or say nothing, must be eliminated. So the scenario writer must bear in mind at all times not what he can put into a picture, but what he can leave out. If each scene has a why and a wherefore and an excuse for being, then you get a perfect continuity.

When I speak of eliminating scenes I do not

Fig. 2. Jeanie Macpherson working on a script with Cecil B. DeMille, ca. 1921 [courtesy of John Belton].

mean that scenes must be cut down to threadbare, straight plot. I find in a great many pictures that the writers deviate from their main theme – that they have two or three themes wandering through the story, which necessarily makes it complicated and hard to follow. If the writer will take a simple single theme, then work up the detail, decorate it with embroidery and lace, every little bit different from the last, but have each bit of trimming pertain directly to the main theme, he will have a much better story. Instead of that, writers branch off with a counterplot or sub-plot which is upsetting and makes the story hard to follow.

Within the next two years I expect to see a school of photodramatists as well known and as distinguished as the dramatists of the speaking stage. Already this school is being developed and established, and within that time it will be set on a firm foundation and photodramatic writers will be given their proper place and will be remembered for their contributions toward this new art.

Originally published in the *Moving Picture World*, 21 July 1917.

How I came to write 'Continuity'

Lloyd Lonergan

Everyone knows what 'continuity' is nowadays, but Edwin Thanhouser is the man who invented it. There wasn't such an animal in 1909, when he started his studio in New Rochelle. Inquiries developed the fact that it was 'all up to' the director.

'Just rely on him', Thanhouser was told. 'A good director will take a company out, see something that will screen well, take it and write a story

around it. Scenarios will be the least of your troubles.'

But the man who is now my boss couldn't see it that way. He had had a long experience in the theatrical game, made a name for himself with his stock company in Milwaukee, and persisted in the belief that the pictures were a form of dramatic art.

'When I had my theatrical company', he said, 'I never told the director, 'Go and put on a play', and trusted to his inventive genius. I selected a manuscript I liked, and he followed it. And I don't see any reason why the same course shouldn't be a success in the motion picture game.'

And that's how I came to 'write continuity', and see it put on the screen at a time when other companies let the directors do everything. I figured out one day that if all the negatives that have [been used to] film[ed] my scripts were laid out in a path six feet wide, they would make a celluloid road from New Rochelle to the shores of the Falkland Islands.

In the early days we didn't go in so much for quick, snappy action. A reel usually ran from 18 to 25 scenes, and people made exits and entrances much as they do on the legitimate stage. A year or so ago I saw a reissue of a picture which, when released some ten years ago created a sensation, but how old fashioned it does appear now. For example, there was one scene that ran this way:

> Set – Corner of drawing room. Woman on with her husband. He bids her farewell and off. Gay Lothario enters. He and wife embrace, show alarm. Lothario goes behind curtain. Husband enters – says he is tired; reclines on lounge. Wife rubs his head; he goes to sleep. Lothario from behind curtains; wife gives him dagger and bids him slay her loving husband. He protests; she insists. He about to do it, then drops knife. He and wife repent and weep.

This was all one scene. Today it would probably be shown in some forty flashes.

I wonder what has become of the old free-lance writers who, seven or eight years ago, used to flood the studios with their offerings. Some of their scripts were so funny that I made notes of them, but not for screen presentation.

Probably the most unusual story of the bunch came from a chap in the Middle West. It narrated the history of an unfortunate family that certainly had trouble in bunches. There was a mortgage on the old homestead, father had lost his job, brother was unjustly in jail, mother had consumption, and it was all up to little ingenue daughter. And *she wrote a motion picture script*. Scenes of suspense while waiting for the returns to come in. And just as the villain was about to put everybody out in the snow, a letter arrived from the film company, enclosing a check that settled all their troubles.

And this supposititious check paid for a one-reel script, for those were the only kind in those days. I often wished that the mythical company was in existence.

Another letter from my collection accompanies an offering from a small town in Pennsylvania. It reads as follows:

> This play is written by my son, Thomas, who is 16 years old. He is too delicate to go out to work and since he had a bad fall two years ago, has been very backward in school. The doctor thinks that in time he may outgrow his feeble mental condition, but in the meanwhile he has turned his attention to motion picture writing, and perhaps there may be a place for him there, so I send you this story which he wrote after supper last evening.
>
> Very respectively,

Another cherished gem of mine is a script which I figure conservatively would cost $250,000 to put on, and it was only written for two reels at that. The Flatiron building is wrecked, there follows a panic among the spectators on Fifth avenue (author indicated that this scene could be taken at night when traffic was light, and there would be nobody to interfere with our supers), there is a collision between two ocean liners, and a few other trifles. As a sample, look at scene 28.

> Scene 28. An observation parlour car on a railroad. Mildred and Henry are on the back platform. He is making love to her. He looks ahead, around side of car, and shrieks as he sees that bridge is open. Mildred, who is looking down the track, cries out that the next train is coming. Henry's train stops. Mildred rushes into his arms, crying, 'Save me! Save me!' as Henry holds her tight, the other engine crashes into the observation car. Henry and Mildred are hurtled into the air, landing on the country road, alongside of the train, just as an auto dashes by. The chauffeur just dodges them.

Yes it is a great business, scenario writing, but it is much more fun to read the stories sent in from the outside – that is, if one has a sense of humour. Originally published in the *Moving Picture World*, 21 July 1917.♠

Film History, Volume 9, pp. 277–289, 1997. Copyright © John Libbey & Company
ISSN: 0892-2160. Printed in Australia

From Rip Van Winkle to Jesus of Nazareth: *thoughts on the origins of the American screenplay*

Patrick Loughney

WK.L. Dickson was not only the world's first motion picture director, he was also the medium's first practical theorist and, at the dawn of motion pictures, he foresaw the coming age of narrative cinema. In an 1894 biography of his then employer Thomas Edison, Dickson devoted an entire chapter to summarising his motion picture camera experiments and describing what he called the 'detached' or miscellaneous subjects he had filmed up to that time. In the final paragraphs of that chapter, Dickson concluded with speculations about the future of movies and stated his belief that complete stage plays would eventually be filmed:

> Hitherto we have limited ourselves to the delineation of detached subjects, but we shall now touch very briefly upon one of the most ambitious schemes, of which these scattered impersonations are but the heralds. *Preparations have long been on foot* to extend the number of actors and to increase the stage facilities, with a view to the presentation of an entire play, set in its appropriate frame. This line of thought may be indefinitely pursued, with ap-

plication to any given phase of outdoor or indoor life which it is desired to reproduce ... No scene, however animated and extensive, but will eventually be within reproductive power.[1] [italics mine]

Dickson understood in early 1894 that it would be some time before either the existing venues of American stage entertainment or the public would be ready for plays adapted to full-length filmed versions. However, the fact that he recognised the competitive feasibility of transforming theatrical works to film – and predicted their eventuality – demonstrates that the concept of using pre-existing written compositions in the making of movies was formulated during, and perhaps before, the first year of commercial cinema production in America.

Dickson might have attempted to develop his

Patrick Loughney is head of the Moving Image section in the M/B/RS division, Library of Congress. Correspondence c/- The Library of Congress, M/B/RS: LM-338, 101 Independence Avenue, Washington, D.C. 20015, USA.

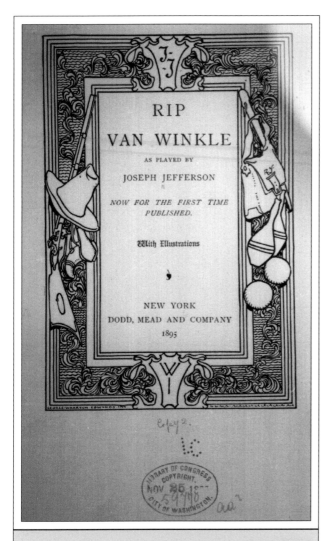

Fig. 1. Cover page of Joseph Jefferson's playscript for *Rip Van Winkle*, published for the first time in 1895 by Dodd, Mead and Co. Jefferson was an early investor in the American Mutoscope and Biograph Company. W.K.L. Dickson had theorised about filming full-length plays as early as 1894, and joining AM&B in 1896 gave him the opportunity to experiment with Jefferson's well-known play.

arranged with Joseph Jefferson – an AM&B stockholder – to produce a Mutoscope version of the famed actor's stage production of *Rip Van Winkle*, which was filmed 'on location' near Jefferson's country home. The 'screenplay' on which the film was based had been published in book form by Jefferson in October 1895.[2] That text, which was introduced as 'now for the first time published', contained stage directions, complete dialogue, plus photographic and other illustrations documenting costume, make-up, scenery and other production elements. Jefferson's publication of the play script was intended, at the time, as the parting commemorative gesture of a famous and beloved actor in the twilight of a long career. However, for present-day researchers seeking clues to the origins of the modern relationship between words and motion pictures, it survives – if not as a true screenplay – then certainly as an important film-related production text from 1896.

Jefferson's edition of *Rip Van Winkle* is among a miscellany of texts in the Library of Congress that relate to the development of motion picture screen writing during the early silent era. The purpose of this article is to consider selected examples that were either adapted to or composed specifically for motion pictures in the early silent period, and to ponder what they say about when, how and why a dependent relationship developed between filmmakers and the written word. A great deal of research and analysis remains to be done before the history of screen texts – in all their permutations as scenarios, scripts, photodramas and screenplays – can be told. Gaps in the historical records of the first production companies and the lack of comprehensive finding aids to surviving scenario and screenplay texts scattered in various archives and libraries hinder the search.[3] Nevertheless, by analysing these texts it is possible to gain selective insights into the general subject area. Nothing of what follows is

'most ambitious schemes' before the close of 1894 but for differences with Edison and his lawyer, Frank Dyer, over recognition of Dickson's inventive contributions to the Kinetograph and Kinetoscope, which caused him to resign and join the rival American Mutoscope & Biograph Company in 1895. It was not until August 1896 that he was able to begin putting his theory into practice. At that time Dickson

meant to suggest a comprehensive, industry-wide understanding of how written compositions came to be a necessary part of the film production process during the early silent era. To the contrary, the surviving texts in the Library of Congress and elsewhere suggest that both the timing of their introduction and the manner in which they were used in the production process differed from company to company in America and, quite likely, also from country to country. Yet, it is possible in this limited space to make useful observations on how some film companies and filmmakers relied on written compositions to further their goals in narrative movie production.

The Library of Congress is informally known to the research community as the 'library of last resort' because it is the nation's largest repository for lost or forgotten publications of the nineteenth and early twentieth centries. Many of those publications came to the LoC as copyright deposits. Among them are a number of motion picture scenarios, dating from the early silent era. In order to convey an idea of the range, form and content of those documents, portions of two different texts discussed in this article – *The Serenade* (Selig, 1905) and *Location d'habits* (Gaumont, 1912) have been reproduced in an appendix, along with a brief history describing how early motion pictures and scenarios were copyrighted after the turn of the century. Also reproduced in the appendix is the exchange of letters between the United States Copyright Office and AM&B in 1904 which are discussed in this article. That correspondence sheds a small but important light on the historical moment at AM&B when the movie scenario came of age as a creative work worthy of recognition and separate copyright protection.

Rip Van Winkle (Dodd, Mead & Co., 1895)

Author: Joseph Jefferson. Text consists of 26 page introduction and 172 pages of dialogue, stage directions and explanatory notes, plus 38 illustrations (photogravures, drawings, etc.).

Rip Van Winkle was the first attempt by an American filmmaker to adapt the complete storyline of a well-

known play to cinema. Short narrative films depicting well-known scenes or incidents from existing theatrical sources had been produced in America since the days of the Kinetoscope, e.g. the five filmed scenes from Charles Hoyt's play *The Milk White Flag* (Edison, 1894). Perhaps the best known example is the April 1896 Edison film *The Kiss*, starring May Irwin and John Rice, which reproduced the climatic comic moment from the hit play *The Widow Jones*. *The Kiss* did not attempt to tell the story of *The Widow Jones* and, like all American comic and dramatic films up to that time, it was more a motion picture vignette than an example of true narrative cinema, in the sense intended by Dickson when he prognosticated the filming of 'an entire play'.

Dickson sought to go much farther with his film version of *Rip Van Winkle*, in spite of the capacity of the Mutoscope flip-card wheels to reproduce motion picture sequences of limited duration. The adaptation was accomplished by editing the play down to a series of eight key narrative scenes. Those scenes were then filmed and printed from individual motion picture film frames to separate pieces of photographic paper, which were then bound in sequential order into Mutoscope wheels – one for each scene. The finished Mutoscope wheels were then distributed as a unit to peepshow parlour venues. The individual scene titles that comprised the whole of *Rip Van Winkle* were: (1) *Rip's Toast*, (2) *Rip Meeting the Dwarf*, (3) *Exit of Rip and the Dwarf*, (4) *Rip Meeting Hudson and Crew*, (5) *Rip's Toast to Hudson and Crew*, (6) *Rip's Twenty Years' Sleep*, (7) *Rip's Awakening* and (8) *Rip Passing over the Mountains*. The production was also distributed, in individual scenes and as a complete film, to venues where the AM&B 'Biograph' projector was installed in 1896–97. A reviewer for the *New York Evening Sun* (7 December 1896), after seeing a projection of *Rip's Toast to Hudson and Crew*, praised the film and also revealed in his comments that Dickson was not alone in recognising the potential of motion pictures to become a new form of dramatic entertainment. 'The marvelous manner in which Joe Jefferson's toast scene from *Rip Van Winkle* is produced by the biograph merely indicates what an important part this photographic machine is going to take in dramatic affairs ...'[4] *Rip Van Winkle* was a hit, but more important for the future of narrative cinema, it proved Dickson's belief that full-length theatrical compositions could be successfully adapted to commercial motion picture entertainments, despite the limitations of the peepshow format.

The Passion:
A miracle play in ten acts

> Author: Salmi Morse. Text consists of 69 pages of dialogue and stage directions. No illustrations.[5]

For a variety of reasons Dickson moved on to other areas of interest soon after *Rip Van Winkle*, but others continued to experiment with the adaptation of stage works to film during a period generally dominated by actuality subjects. The next important step in the development of the American narrative film was taken by Richard Hollaman and Albert Eaves with their 1898 Eden Musee production *The Passion Play of Oberammergau*. This production is the most interesting anomaly in the story of early American movie writing because it was actually based on a script written in 1879. It is the *Ur*-text in the history of the American movie screenplay. The original composition was a play script called *The Passion*, which was authored by a small-time California playwright named Salmi Morse.[6] The story of *The Passion* and how Morse's play script came to be used in the making of the Hollaman and Eaves production was first told by Terry Ramsaye in *A Million and One Nights*.[7] For our purposes, it stands alongside Rip Van Winkle as a prime example of a fully formed dramatic composition which, by virtue of its format and production information, served as a ready blueprint for a motion picture production. *The Passion Play of Oberammergau* more fully realised the potential of its written source material and advanced the development of American narrative film because it was produced, edited and exhibited as a complete projected film, rather than the episodic peepshow format of *Rip Van Winkle*. The length of the play text, at 69 pages, also allowed

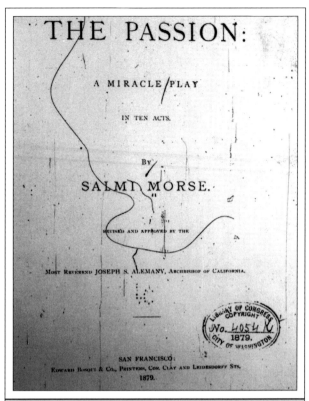

Fig. 2. Cover page of Salmi Morse's *The Passion*, first published in San Franscisco in 1879 and copyrighted in the same year. Morse's efforts to produce the play in New York during the early 1880s failed, and his script became the property of one of the play's backers, Albert Eaves. In 1898 Eaves became a partner of Richard Hollaman, manager of the Eden Musee theatre in New York, in the production of *The Passion Play of Oberammergau*, which was based on Morse's long-forgotten script.

the erstwhile filmmakers Hollaman and Eaves, who had no prior experience with narrative filmmaking, to undertake the production of a movie of extraordinary duration for the time. The length of the completed *Passion Play* was about 1900 feet and when projected ran for almost twenty minutes. When the eight individual scenes of *Rip Van Winkle* were edited together and re-released in 35 mm by AM&B in 1903, the print length was 200 feet.[8]

Six AM&B scenarios, 1904–05

> Authors: Frank Marion and Wallace McCutcheon. Texts: one printed version of *The Suburbanite* and five typescripts for *The Chicken*

Thief, Tom, Tom the Piper's Son, The Nihilists, Wanted; A Dog and *The Wedding*.[9]

If the nineteenth century play script format was the starting point for experimental narrative films, then the scenario – a descriptive work without dialog – was the textual format that served the early need of early filmmakers for brief compositions that could be easily adapted to short narrative films. The use of such original compositions in the making of narrative movies may have been a routine practice in one or more American companies as early as 1897. Moreover, it is possible that professional writers were being hired by then to produce and direct films because of their skills at creating narrative ideas appropriate to short films. Supporting this view is a profile of Roy L. McCardell, published in the *Moving Picture World* in 1912 under the title 'The First Photoplaywright', which identified him as:

> ... the first man in America hired to write plots for motion pictures. It was in 1897 that the Biograph Company needed the services of someone to write the fifty foot subjects for the Biograph and Mutoscope. Up to that time anyone around a studio wrote the plays, but the demand for mutoscope pictures...was strong and McCardell, who was then on the staff of the New York Telegraph, was put on the staff as author, editor, producer and press man. He has been at it ever since and sells from two to four scripts a week.[10]

None of McCardell's nineneeth-century scripts are known to exist but this early tantalising reference certainly makes him a candidate worthy of further investigation. One piece of evidence that supports his claim that AM&B was using scenarios in 1897 survives in the form of a Mutoscope advertising card for the film *Three Jolly Girls*.[11] At the bottom of the card, in small type, is the following notice:

> $5.00 for an idea. The Proprietors will pay $5.00 for any suggestion of a good scene adopted and used by them in the Biograph or Mutoscope. Scenes submitted should be minutely described. Comedy scenes are preferred. In case two or more persons submit the same suggestion the money will be paid to the party whose suggestion is first received.

Address all suggestions to the American Mutoscope Co., 841 Broadway, New York City.

In spite of these references, no examples of original AM&B scenarios are known to this author before a series of texts in the Library of Congress from the period 1904–05. Beginning in November 1904, AM&B copyrighted and released a sequence of films over the next seven months for which it also registered original scenarios. Those productions and their release dates are *The Suburbanite* (28 November 1904), *The Chicken Thief* (27 December 1904), *Tom, Tom the Piper's Son* (15 March 1905), *The Nihilists* (27 March 1905), *Wanted; A Dog* (17 April 1905) and *The Wedding* (22 May 1905).[12] Why Biograph managers copyrighted the scenarios for their narrative releases during that period is unknown, but the texts themselves reveal important clues about why and how they were used in the production process of that day. The first to be registered was *The Suburbanite*, which was actually copyrighted in the form of the printed Biograph Bulletin no. 37.[13] The remaining five documents in the series were registered in typescript form. None contain dialogue. *The Nihilists* typescript typifies the general format and style of the AM&B scenarios delivered to the Copyright Office over 90 years ago.

The Nihilists is a dramatic narrative about an incident of injustice committed against a noble Polish family by a local Russian ruler during the 1905 revolution, and the efforts of the nobleman's children to gain revenge by joining an underground anarchist group. The cover page announces the title and follows with the statement, 'An Original American Drama in Seven Scenes, based on Recent Incidents in Russia'. Next, is a credit line in capital letters announcing Frank J. Marion and Wallace McCutcheon as the authors, followed by a statement declaring the work to be the 'property' of AM&B. Page two lists the cast of characters: eleven principal roles and an unnumbered group of minor roles described as, 'Nihilists of the extremist section, cossacks, jailers, political prisoners, coachmen, gate tenders, servants of the Governor's palace, etc'. After the cast list is information about the historical period and geographical location to be depicted in the film, 'The Period is today. The Costumes, Properties and Scenic Effects are char-

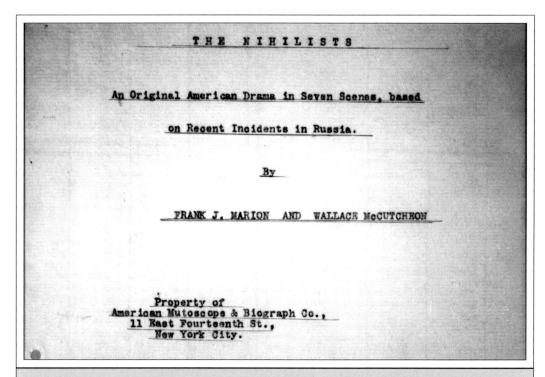

Fig. 3. Title page of *The Nihilists*, written by Frank J. Marion and Wallace McCutcheon, and copyrighted in 1905 in two formats by the American Mutoscope and Biograph Company – as a scenario and as a motion picture. *The Nihilists* was one of a series of six productions copyrighted in this manner by AM&B from November 1904 through May 1905.

acteristic of Warsaw, Poland at the present time'. Page three describes in order the locations where each scene in the film is to take place. From the cover page we know that there are seven scenes in the production, however page three actually lists eleven separate incidents to be filmed. There are eleven scenes because scenes four and eight each require three separate sets to be constructed or outdoor locations to be found and, thus, extra camera set-ups. The location for scene one, for example, is described as, 'Interior of the dining-room of a high-class private residence of Warsaw'.

Of the sixteen total pages in *The Nihilists* text, the first two (after the cover page) are devoted to information necessary to the pre-production work of casting the film and assembling the proper 'costumes, properties and scenic effects' in preparation for the filming date. The remaining thirteen pages provide additional specifics on set and costume design. At this point, the document shifts emphasis

from preparatory instructions to the presentation of detailed scene-by-scene descriptions that explain the actions to be depicted and how they are to be staged. The first of these 'production information' pages (page four) begins with a statement of the various time periods to be depicted in the film's eight separate scenes.

THE ACTION is not continuous. One day is supposed to separate the first and second scenes. The third scene is supposed to have occurred on the evening of the first day. The first part of the fourth scene occurs on the third day, and the following two scenes a month later. The fifth scene occurs on an evening a month later, after the news of the father's death has reached the children. Scene six occurs at consecutive intervals in the daytime a week after the action of scene five. Scene seven occurs on an evening a month after the action of scene six.

For each scene thereafter, two distinct types of information are given that seem to have been written primarily to help the director and cast more clearly understand how they were to interpret the plot. The first type supplies specifics of set design and briefly describes how the action is to be staged, as in these instructions for scene two:

The dungeon of a military prison; the walls of heavy stonework. Chains fastened to the wall at the back centre. Stage clear, except for a small plain table and several chairs.

The second type describes the actions to be performed by the cast and realised on film by the director:

The old man appears before a hasty court-martial presided over by the Governor himself, and is condemned without a hearing. At the Governor's orders, he is seized by a couple of burly Cossacks, stripped until his back is bare, and is then chained to the wall, with his arms above his head. He is then cruelly knouted with the many-thonged whip in use in Russian prisons. He faints under the awful punishment, and is hurriedly released and flung half dead upon the table, from which he falls, writhing in agony, to the floor.

The completed film version of *The Nihilists*, with the opening title sequence and intertitles for each scene, measured 840 feet in length. The surviving film copy in the Paper Print collection shows a production that adhered very closely to the scenario in every detail, including an interesting explosive special effect achieved by double exposure.

The Serenade (1905)

Author: William N. Selig. Four scenes. Text: 13-page typescript, with dialogue and limited stage directions. (See appendix)

William Selig's *The Serenade* demonstrates that at least one other American producer was using pre-existing narrative texts as the basis of film productions in 1905.[14] The typescript registered by Selig on 1 May 1905 differs greatly in format from the scenarios copyrighted by AM&B in that it contains dialogue. As such, it is much more a true script than a scenario, suggesting that the scenario/screenplay texts used in the production of narrative films in 1905 varied greatly in form and content from one American studio to another. For example, *The Serenade* text is a twelve-page document that contains complete dialogue sequences for each of the five characters. Stage directions are de-emphasised and limited to brief phrases scattered throughout the text. Instructions for set and costume designs and additional background information that might have been useful to the director and cast are nonexistent. The construction of *The Nihilists* text is quite different. Although sixteen pages long it contains no dialogue; emphasis is focused instead on giving the director and the cast the clearest possible plot description and directions on how to transform the narrative action from words to moving images. Of the two documents, *The Nihilists* is more directed in its purpose and more sophisticated in its development as a composition written to facilitate a motion picture production.

The surviving AM&B camera operator's record book shows that filming of *The Nihilists* was completed in one or two days, beginning or ending on 28 February.[15] An analysis of the Biograph Bulletins for the 1904–05 period reveals that, beginning with the release of *The Moonshiners* in July 1904, AM&B began to increase both the frequency of production and the length of its comic and dramatic films. What the paper print copy of *The Nihilists* makes clear is that, by following the scenario, the cast and crew were able to efficiently complete a complicated production in a relatively short period of time. Prior to filming *The Moonshiners*, AM&B had imported for distribution in the United States the Warwick production *Marie Antoinette*. This film consisted of nine scenes and it had a release length of 575 feet. *The Nihilists*, completed one year later, included a total of eleven different camera set-ups, was filmed in one or two days and its release length was 840 feet.

The trend of increasing complexity and length after *Marie Antoinette* suggests that AM&B began reacting to the trend among foreign companies toward the production of longer narrative films and decided to follow suit. One way of achieving that goal might have been to integrate a more specialised scenario format into its production process by mid-1904, as a better way of fixing budgets, scheduling personnel, arranging costumes and set construction, hiring appropriate actors, and planning sales campaigns. All of those tasks had to be planned in an orderly sequence for AM&B to sustain a profitable production and release schedule, and the specific scenario format devised by Marion and McCutcheon seems to have been essential to that process.

One can imagine how the AM&B staff might have functioned on the morning in late February or early March, when production of *The Nihilists* began: actors arriving at the appointed time to find costumes waiting and sets constructed; the director, having blocked out the scenes, waiting to give instructions on filming the first scene; film stock ordered and camera operator, lights and other equipment ready; the sales department busily composing the text of the Biograph Bulletin to be sent on deadline to the printer, in order to get the advertising information out to theatre owners as quickly as possible, and so on. In this context, *The Nihilists* – as text and movie – signifies that two important developments in American commercial film production had taken place by late 1904: (1) an effective scenario format for use in the making of longer narrative films up to one reel in length had been developed, and (2) the importance of starting with specially written texts as the basis for organising regular film productions had been recognised by the management of one of America's leading film companies.

While these texts are evidence that at least those two companies were using scenario/screenplay texts in 1904–05, their existence does not tell us when AM&B, Selig and other American companies first began using such works in planning and producing movies on a regular basis. AM&B may well have been using simple scenarios as early as 1897, as suggested by McCardell's testimony and other circumstantial evidence, but it is unlikely that their compositional format was as complex as the Marion-McCutcheon scenarios registered in 1904–05. Among the surviving ephemera in the Copyright Office archives is a brief exchange of legal correspondence that took place between AM&B and the Copyright Office in 1904, relating to the registration of *The Suburbanite*.[16] The central

issue of that correspondence turned on AM&B's attempt to register its printed advertising bulletin for *The Suburbanite* as a dramatic composition. The Copyright Office, thinking that the bulletin was not a true dramatic composition because it lacked dialogue, replied to AM&B that it would be more proper to register the work as a 'book' than a play. AM&B's lawyers, citing appropriate precedents, successfully argued that the absence of dialogue did not disqualify registering the work as a dramatic composition. The timing of that exchange may signify the period when the movie scenario formally (and legally?) emerged as an accepted and necessary creative part of the film production process, at least at AM&B. Two questions raised by those letters are: Why was AM&B management motivated to copyright movie scenarios at that time, in addition to the films? and, Why did AM&B not register scenario texts before 1904, if they had been part of the production process since 1897?

A possible answer might be that, prior to the 1904–05 period, the use of scenarios by AM&B filmmakers was so informal, and their compositional format so undeveloped, that they were considered to be neither worthy of creative recognition, apart from the films made from them, nor unique enough to be protected from piracy by copyright registration. Something happened in 1904 that changed the way AM&B produced narrative films. In his biography, Billy Bitzer refers vaguely to a series of personnel changes begun after 1903, including one manager who tried to improve the efficiency of studio operations.[17] Was the development of an improved scenario format part of an effort to improve operational efficiency? Evidence for such a change may be reflected in the new format for the Biograph Bulletins that first appeared for *Marie Antoinette* on 23 February 1904. The new format included much more descriptive information than the old and was also used for all the major AM&B narrative productions after *The Moonshiners* up to *The Suburbanite* in November 1904: *The Moonshiners* (28 July 1904), *The Pioneers* (5 August 1904), *Personal* (15 August 1904), *The Widow and the Only Man* (29 August 1904) and *The Lost Child* (26 October 1904). It is possible that the source of the extended descriptive information used in the new format bulletins from *The Moonshiners* through *The Lost Child* was recycled from the scenarios on which the films were based. That is what happened for *The Chicken Thief, Tom, Tom the Piper's Son, The Nihilists, Wanted; A Dog* and *The Wedding*; the descriptive text incorporated in the Biograph Bulletins for each of those films was taken verbatim from the copyrighted scenarios. The question here is did it become standard practice, as an efficiency measure of the AM&B front office beginning in February 1904, to gain double benefit from scenario texts by also using them in the production of advertising literature? If so, then the Biograph Bulletins that were printed during the company's history should be more carefully examined as possible sources of surviving original scenario compositions.

Location d'habits (Gaumont, 1912)

> Author: René d'Héry. Typewritten text: 5 pages with stage directions and dialogue.

Little is known about this text other than that it is one of 40 compositions copyrighted on 21 June 1912 by the Gaumont Company of Flushing, New York. All but two of the works are in French and all contain dialogue and stage directions in a similar format.[18] The presumption that these texts were written as screenplays is based on the fact that they were copyrighted by the American branch of the Gaumont Company, which was located in Flushing, New York in 1912. The word 'Flushing' is stamped in bold letters on the upper left-hand corner of the typescript for *Location d'habits* and several others in the series. A check of the American Film Institute database shows no known copy of this or any of the 39 other titles in the collections of the United States film archives. A cross-check of the 1912 titles listed in *Gaumont 90 ans de cinéma* reveals an exact match for one title (*Armoire normandie*) and possible variant forms of a number of others.[19] It is possible that some of these screenplays were purchased from the authors and never filmed or that they were filmed and the titles were changed prior to release. If they were produced and released in the United States it is certain that the resulting films would have been retitled.

Location d'habits is a farce comedy about two rural characters who are invited to the city home of a noble woman, and the misadventures they have while trying to dress properly for high society. The film produced from this text would most probably have been no more than one half reel in length. The style of the 1912 Gaumont text is similar to Selig's 1905 script for *The Serenade*. Both texts intermix dialogue and stage directions and depend on the stage business and energy of the actors to put across the narrative humour. The existence of *Location d'habits* and its companion screenplays is an indicator that the search for pre-production texts from the early silent era needs to be broadened to include foreign language materials that relate to the many European companies that produced and distributed films in the United States market before World War 1.

From the Manger to the Cross or Jesus of Nazareth (Kalem, 1912)

> Author: Gene Gauntier. Printed text: 29 pages, consisting of 5 page scene synopsis, 3 page description of 'light plot' and props, and 20 pages of dialogue and stage directions.

From the Manger to the Cross is generally recognised today as a breakthrough in the achievement of realism on the early American screen. It is historically important specifically because of its length, subject matter, and the fact that it was filmed on location in Palestine with an international cast. It is also of significance to the history of movie screenwriting because of the photoplay authored by Gene Gauntier, who played the role of Mary in the production. Gauntier was one of the leading actresses of the day but she was also an experienced scenario author, dating to her employment at AM&B in 1906. Her most famous screenwriting credit was for the scenario used in the making of the 1907 Kalem production *Ben Hur*. That unauthorised adaptation of *Ben Hur* became the subject of a landmark legal case between Kalem and Harper Bros., the book's publisher, which was ultimately settled by a United States Supreme Court decision against Kalem in 1911. The lawsuit itself is important because of the impetus it gave to formalising the profession of screenwriting after 1907, when the suit was initiated. Even though it took four years before the case was ultimately resolved, film producers realised almost immediately that they could no longer adapt copy-righted plays, novels, etc., to motion pictures without paying authors and publishers for the privilege. The least expensive way for film companies to protect themselves from potential lawsuits was to either purchase or write their own narrative texts and use them as the direct source for their film productions.

From the Manger to the Cross may be the earliest known example of a fully developed modern American screenplay. Like the AM&B productions of 1904–05, *Manger* was copyrighted as both a film (23 October 1912) and a dramatic composition (2 December 1912). Publishing and distributing the scenario seems to have been part of Kalem's promotion campaign for the film. The copyrighted text has two title pages, the first of which has a large publicity photo, depicting the scene of Jesus recruiting the apostles James and John; the Kalem logo; and the following advertising blurb:

> This Kalem Masterpiece was produced in authentic locations in Palestine and Egypt at a cost of $100,000, requiring the services of forty-two skilled actors for the principal parts portrayed, hundreds of natives and camels, and consuming over three months in photographing.

The second simply lists the standard publication information: title, description ('A Drama in Five Acts'), author and copyright notice.

From the Manger to the Cross

or

JESUS OF NAZARETH

THE CALLING OF JAMES AND JOHN
(The Sea of Galilee)

This Kalem Masterpiece was produced in authentic locations in Palestine and Egypt at a cost of $100,000., requiring the services of forty-two skilled actors for the principal parts portrayed, hundreds of natives and camels, and consuming over three months in photographing.

(COPYRIGHTED 1912 BY KALEM COMPANY)

KALEM COMPANY 235 W. 23rd St NEW YORK

Fig. 4. Cover page of the printed edition of Gene Gauntier's screenplay *From the Manger to the Cross*, which was published and copyrighted by Kalem in 1912. Gauntier's text demonstrates that, at least by 1912, the American screenplay had achieved a fully realised form in which character dialogue was balanced with specific information on stage directions, set designs, props, costumes, and other elements necessary in creating a film production.

The format of Gauntier's 'photoplay' is quite sophisticated compared to other scenario/screenplay documents with earlier dates found in the Library of Congress. It is similar in compositional format to the Marion-McCutcheon scenarios, in that it concentrates on providing clear instructions for use in planning and filming the production, and, like Selig's *The Serenade*, it includes dialogue. However, the format of Gauntier's text is more structured and better designed as a film production tool. Every aspect of the information provided by Gauntier is more detailed and balanced in the sense that it addresses the needs of all members of the production team: the director, camera operator, electrician, set designer, carpenter, prop master and cast. It is a model of conciseness that begins (after the two title pages) on page three with a synopsis, listing a brief description of the location for each of the 75 scenes in the production. Scenes one, two and three, for example, are described as, 'A Hill overlooking a Palestine Village, The Bedroom of Mary, The Carpenter Shop of Joseph' and so on. Pages six through eight contain detailed scene-by-scene descriptions of the required lighting directions and props. The remaining twenty pages focus on the narrative to be filmed and are evenly divided between dialogue and stage directions, which are precise and indicate the directional movements of the main actors in every scene, as in this example for act one, scene three:

> Street in Nazareth, showing doorway of Joseph's carpenter shop; women pass by, going to and from the well for water; huge jugs on their heads. Joseph discovered working. Enter Mary, right upper entrance; passes diagonally across to left first entrance, turns, smiles at Joseph, drops eyes and exits.

A viewing of the surviving film shows that the corresponding scene was directed and performed exactly as described. The surviving paper print fragments that accompanied the 23 October film registration show that only two additional scenes not previously written in the screenplay were either improvised on location or edited into the final release version.

Producung *From the Manger to the Cross* was an unusually ambitious gamble for the Kalem company, in part because the life of Christ was a subject avoided by American film companies after 1898 and partly because of the cost of filming on location in the Holy Land. It is doubtful that such an enterprise would have been undertaken without careful prior planning by the Kalem management, including a well- written screenplay to be produced when they arrived. It is a meaningful coincidence that one of the founding managers of the Kalem company was Frank J. Marion, who co-authored *The Nihilists* and the other AM&B scenarios of 1904–05. It is very likely that he understood the importance of having a carefully prepared text before embarking on such a risky production and encouraged Gauntier to write it. Marion may also have made the crucial decision to support Gauntier's direction, delivered in a note at the bottom of page five, to produce the film on location.

> N.B. The dramatist in this work aims to give an accurate and reverential picture of the leading events in the Life of Jesus of Nazareth. To this end if the drama be shown by means of motion pictures, wherever possible each scene is to be enacted in the exact location as pointed out by leading authorities.

From the Manger to the Cross does not usually appear on anyone's list of the greatest films of the early silent era, but it is quite likely that it stayed in continuous distribution longer than any other film produced before 1920, including *The Birth of a Nation*. Old projection prints were still being circulated to churches and other religious venues as late as the 1940s. It's popularity was due undoubtedly to the use of Holy Land locations and the solid dramatic portrayal of the life of Christ. Credit is also due to the screenplay by Gene Gauntier.

There is much internal evidence in the surviving films of the early silent era to suggest that the use of adapted and original texts flourished simultaneously across the spectrum of companies that comprised the American film industry of the period between *Rip Van Winkle* and *From the Manger to the Cross*. The interaction between words and movies in the early silent era was dynamic and complex, and narrative works written for a wide range of entertainments lent themselves readily to film adaptations. Within that spectrum, as the public taste for longer narrative films developed, the scenario/screenplays we have examined indicate that there was a concerted effort by some filmmakers to develop special text formats to increase the efficiency of film production. The texts we have discussed here gauge some small portions of what was achieved between 1896 and 1912.

The progress apparent in the refinement of the

motion picture screenplay format in the seven years between *The Nihilists* and *From the Manger to the Cross* seems to have been substantial, especially compared to what we know of film-related texts prior to 1904. *The Nihilists* consists of sixteen pages of text that resulted in the production of a film less than one reel in length with a running time of approximately fourteen minutes. *From the Manger to the Cross* is 29 pages in length and from it was produced a five-reel motion picture, measuring approximately 4800 feet with a running time of 80 minutes.[20] Gene Gauntier may not have been the first writer to compose a screenplay in the precise format found in *From the Manger to the Cross*, but her text is the earliest such work discovered among the copyright records in the Library of Congress. It is therefore important because it marks the end of a seventeen-year period, dating from Jefferson's 1895 text for *Rip Van Winkle*, in which it can be demonstrated that American narrative filmmakers moved from the adaptation of pre-existing stage scripts to the use, at least in this one instance, of texts specially written for the production of multi-reel movies.

It has been my goal in this paper to make what I hope are some useful observations about the origins of the relationship between early American filmmakers and the written word during the early silent era. I have also sought to draw attention to some unusual texts in the collections of the Library of Congress that are important to the history of early American narrative cinema. All are worthy of more detailed analysis than they have received here, particularly in comparison to the surviving films made from them. ♠

Notes

1. W.K.L. Dickson and Antonia Dickson, *The Life and Inventions of Thomas Alva Edison* (New York: Thomas Y. Crowell, 1894), 318–319.

2. Joseph Jefferson, *Rip Van Winkle* (New York: Dodd, Mead & Co., 1895). The Library of Congress copy is in the general book collection under the call number PS2068.A37J4. The play premiered in Washington, DC in 1862 and Jefferson performed it countless thousands of times. It became his signature piece and was one of the most popular American plays of the later half of the nineteenth century.

3. Depending on when and how they were acquired, those in the Library of Congress are located in the general book collection and the separate collections of the Copyright Office, Motion Picture (M/B/RS), Manuscript and Rare Book divisions.

4. Kemp Niver, *Biograph Bulletins 1896–1908* (Los Angeles: Locare Research Group, 1971), 21. Contemporary review reproduced in this publication.

5. Salmi Morse, *The Passion: A Miracle Play in Ten Acts* (San Francisco: Edward Bosqui & Co., 1879). Library of Congress copy exists on microfilm; call number PN6120.R4 M6.

6. Alan Nielsen, *The Great Victorian Sacrilege* (Jefferson, N.C: McFarland & Co., 1991), 230ff. Nielsen gives an excellent historical account of how one of Morse's former investors, Albert Eaves, kept the script and costumes from a failed New York production of the play in the early 1880s, and later teamed with Richard Hollaman and actor Frank Russell to produce a film version, using the script and costumes, in 1898. For Nielsen's discussion of the similarities between Salmi's work and the film, see his notes to chapter 12, 278.

7. Terry Ramsaye, *A Million And One Nights* (New York: Simon & Schuster, 1926), 368ff.

8. Niver, *Biograph Bulletins 1896–1908*, 82.

9. Original copies in the collection of the Moving Image Section, Room LM–338, Library of Congress.

10. *Moving Picture World*, vol. 14, no. 11 (14 December 1912), 1075.

11. Reproduced in Niver, *Biograph Bulletins 1896–1908*, 24. Original in collection of Moving Image Section, Room LM–338, Library of Congress.

12. Both the movies and the scenarios are in the collections of the Moving Image Section, Room LM–338, Library of Congress.

13. See appendix.

14. See appendix for sample pages of *The Serenade* text.

15. The AM&B camera operator's register in the collections of the Museum of Modern Art Department of Film and Television indicates that the production date was 28 February and that the exterior scenes were shot in Grantwood, N.J. The much more extensive interior scenes would have been filmed in Manhattan at the 14th Street studio and it is therefore probable that filming occurred over a two day period, including either 27 February or 1 March.

16. See appendix.

17. Billy Bitzer, *Billy Bitzer – His Story* (New York: Farrar, Straus & Giroux, 1971), 50.

18. See a selection of this text reproduced in the appendix.

19. Philippe d'Hugues and Dominique Muller, *Gaumont 90 ans de cinéma* (Paris: La Cinémathèque Française), 204.

20. A 35 mm print of 840 feet projected at a rate of sixteen frames per second (fps) equals a running time of fourteen minutes. The surviving print of *From the Manger to the Cross* in the Library of Congress measures 4780 feet, which translates to a running time of 80 minutes, if projected at sixteen fps.

Film History, Volume 9, pp. 290–299, 1997. Copyright © John Libbey & Company
ISSN: 0892-2160. Printed in Australia

Appendix: Selected examples of early scenario/screenplays in the Library of Congress

Patrick Loughney

S cattered throughout the archives and libraries of America and Europe are many fragments of the history of writing for movies. The majority remain unrecognised for what they are and no systematic effort has yet been made to identify, catalogue and describe them. The main reasons are that corporate records of the early production companies are generally lost or widely scattered, and historians have not yet begun to thoroughly investigate when the use of pre-existing or specially created written materials was introduced into the industrial filmmaking process. Telltale fragments of the early relationship between words and cinema do exist, however, and some day enough will be collected to tell much more than we now know about how and when early producers came to rely on written source materials as key tools in regularising the mass production of movies.

The three following examples suggest the variety of documentation that exists. Each originated with a different film producer at different times and places in the United States. The common fate eventually shared by them is that they were originally acquired by the United States Copyright Office and all are now part of the permanent collection of the Library of Congress Moving Image Section. Before proceeding further, however, it is important to digress for a brief explanation of how early American film producers dealt with the limitations of nineteenth century copyright law, and to understand a few details of how the bureaucratic record keeping procedures of the United States Copyright Office developed at the beginning of this century. Arcane though it undeniably is, this digression is nevertheless important to fully understanding these documents and their relationship to film history.

Turn-of-the-century procedures of the US Copyright Office

The purpose of copyright law is to protect the intellectual property inherent in creative works that are mechanically reproduced for wide-spread distribution and sale. By the end of the nineteenth century, the United States Copyright law formally recognised the existence of copyrightable activities in the following format areas: books, periodicals (newspaper, magazines, etc.), musical compositions (sheet music), maps and charts, engravings, lithographs and photographs. (Works created or invented in other forms were then, and still are, covered separately by a law and Department of Commerce bureaucracy governing patents and trademarks.) Though the Copyright law defined categories for copyrightable works, the Copyright

Office – the bureaucracy charged with recording and keeping track of all things copyrighted – made no distinction or classification among formats in the sequential *registration numbers* it routinely assigned to items deposited before 1900. That purely numeric system made it difficult for Copyright Office clerks to tabulate at the end of each year how many works had been registered in the various copyrightable formats (books, engravings, photographs, etc.). Being a government agency with a mandate to report on the nation's copyright activities to Congress every year, the keeping of those statistics was (and is) a very serious matter to the Copyright Office. The rapid growth of copyright registrations throughout the 1890s forced the Copyright Office to make changes to ease its accounting burden. (During the period 1 July 1898 to 1 July 1899, the Copyright Office processed 59,217 individual registrations.)

By 1900 the number of copyright applications had grown so voluminous and their variety so complex that the Copyright Office tried to clarify matters for the public and its own staff by establishing four alphabetical sub-categories or classes for copyright deposits: Books (Class A), Periodicals (Class B), Musical Compositions (Class C) and Dramatic Compositions (Class D). All copyright deposits received in 1900 were registered in one of these classes. The change proved successful and additional classes were added in 1901 to further refine the categorisation process for the other distinct copyrightable formats: Maps or Charts (Class E), Engravings, Cuts or Prints (Class F), Chromos or Lithographs (Class G) and Photographs (Class H).[1]

For materials registered without complication, the copyright process of 1901 was straightforward: 1) an author or composer mailed a deposit to the Copyright Office in Washington, DC with the appropriate 50-cent fee and a completed application form; 2) the deposit item and application were examined by a clerk to determine the item's format and to verify that the claimant had applied for registration in the correct category; 3) an exclusive registration number was assigned within the appropriate format class; 4) the deposit item and related paperwork were filed in the Copyright Office archive; and 5) formal notification of completed registration was returned in a few weeks by mail to the claimant. When a misunderstanding occurred

between a claimant and the Copyright Office, as in the case of the attempted registration by the American Mutoscope & Biograph Company (AM&B) of *The Suburbanite* as a 'dramatic composition', the copyright process was delayed while correspondence ensued to straighten out the problem. That routine exchange of correspondence from 1904 sheds an important light on the earliest verifiable period when the AM&B company was using some form of scenario/screenplay in the making of movies.

The Suburbanite (AM&B, 1904)

What makes *The Suburbanite* so interesting to the discussion of early scenario writing is that AM&B submitted the work for separate copyright in two distinct formats, once as a 'photograph' in Class H on 11 November 1904, and the second time as a 'dramatic composition' in Class D on 25 November 1904. The photographic registration (Class H52864) – now part of the Library of Congress Paper Print collection and viewable by researchers in the form of a 16 mm print – is a farce comedy about the travails of life in the suburbs of New York. AM&B was the claimant for both registrations, though the application form for the dramatic composition (Class D5895), which has a block for such information, identifies Frank J. Marion as the author.[2] The difference between the two deposits is that the Class H registration was uncontested, whereas the item submitted for the Class D registration occasioned a letter from the Register of Copyrights, Thorvald Solberg, questioning the category to which AM&B had applied for registration and suggesting that Class A (books) might be more appropriate than Class D (dramatic compositions). Solberg's reason for doubting the relevance of the second claim for *The Suburbanite* in Class D was that the work contained no character dialogue.

The following series of three letters between Solberg and AM&B's lawyers (Kerr, Page & Cooper) began on 1 December 1904 and closed with a final letter from Solberg dated 9 December:

Item 1: [Transcription of letter from Register of Copyrights to AM &B.]

The Library of Congress December 1 1904
Copyright Office
Washington, DC

Gentlemen:

By request of the Librarian of Congress, I have the honor to acknowledge receipt of your application for entry of what you term a 'dramatic composition' entitled 'The Suburbanite'.

The article sent consists of a four-page folder describing a series of moving pictures. The term 'dramatic composition' as used in the copyright law has the ordinary meaning of that term, that is, a play consisting of dialogue and action. Your article is *[apparently]* not a dramatic composition as the term is used in the law, and it would not be permissible to make entry as a dramatic composition.[3] Possibly protection could be secured for the article if registered as a 'book', and if you wish such entry made and will write a letter authorizing the necessary amendment to your application, the matter will receive prompt attention. Your remittance of 50 cents is held as number 36849 awaiting your reply, which please send in the inclosed envelope.

Respectfully,
[signed]   Thorvald Solberg
Register of Copyrights

American Mutoscope & Biograph Co.
11 East 14th Street
New York City

Item 2: [Transcription of letter from Drury W. Cooper, on behalf of AM&B, to the Register of Copyrights.]

Law offices of Kerr, Page & Cooper
Singer Building, 149 Broadway
New York City   December 6th, 1904

To the Hon. Librarian of Congress, Washington, DC.

Sir:

The American Mutoscope & Biograph Co. have referred to us for consideration and answer your letter No. 36,849, with reference to their application for copyright registration as a dramatic composition of 'The Suburba-

nite'.

As we understand, your position is that the term 'dramatic composition' as used in the copyright law means a play consisting of dialogue and action, and that the composition in question is not dramatic in that it has no dialogue. We take issue with this position, and submit that the article in question is a dramatic composition in the meaning of the law, and that a dramatic composition does not necessarily require dialogue.

In *Barnes vs. Miner*, 122 Fed. Rep., 480, 490, the Court (Ray, Judge) says:
'The words "dramatic or musical composition" used in the suit as applied in this case must be held to include only those representations and exhibitions, with or without prefatory and accompanying words, which tend at least to promote the progress of science and useful arts'.

Referring to the composition in question, it is obviously within the definition of this case. It is a representation or exhibition consisting of 7 scenes and 16 characters. The action is to depict the story described in the composition itself. It is the sole purpose of the composition that this narrative or story shall be represented dramatically by action, posture and gesture. Classing such representation as a useful art, it is unquestioned that it is intended to promote that art by the creation and exhibition of 'The Suburbanite'.

Again, in the case of Daly vs. Palmer, 2 Fed. Cas. 3553; 6 Blatchf. 264, it was said:
'To act in the sense of the statute is to represent as real by countenance, voice, or gesture that which is not real. A character in a play goes through with a series of events on the stage without speaking, if such be his part in the play, is none the less an actor in it than one who, in addition to motions and gestures, uses his voice. A pantomime is a species of theatrical entertainment, in which the whole action is represented by gesticulation without the use of words. A written work consisting wholly of directions set in order for conveying the ideas of the author on a stage or public place by means of characters who represent the narrative wholly by action is as much a dramatic composition designed or suited for public repre-

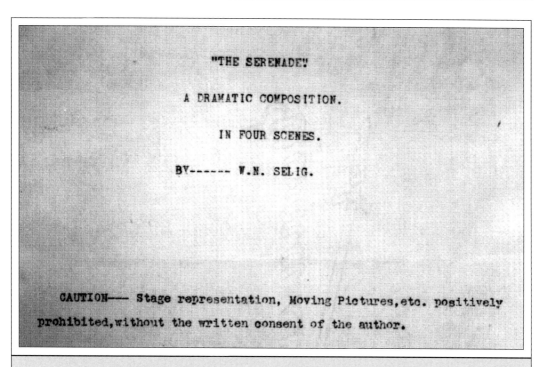

Fig. 1. Typescript cover page for *The Serenade*, deposited for copyright in 1904 by William Selig. Selig's manuscript contains complete dialogue for all the characters and minimises stage directions and other instructions, unlike the contemporary documents registered by AM&B.

sentation as if language or dialogue were used in it to convey some of the ideas.'

'Movement, gesture, and facial expression, which address the eye only, are as much a part of the dramatic composition as is the spoken language which addresses the ear only; and that part of the written composition which gives direction for the movement and gesture, is as much a part of the composition, and protected by the copyright, as in the language prescribed to be uttered by the character.'

See also *Daly vs. Webster*, 56 Fed. Rep., 483.

If the purpose of a dramatic composition is to represent as real that which is not real, its fulfillment will be found in the composition which our clients have submitted for protection.

Other cases might be cited, but the forgoing suffice.

See also *Drone on Copyright*, 588, 593.

Something of novelty may be presented by the fact that this particular dramatic composition has been photographed in a series of living

pictures, and is susceptible of being represented thereby. That however, is true of substantially every drama, or at least of every drama which depends in large part for its portrayal upon an appeal to the eye rather than the ear, and does not affect the author's right to registration or to protection from unauthorized representation by that or other means.

We submit that the certificate of registration should be granted.

Very respectfully,
[signed] Drury W. Cooper

Item 3: [Transcription of letter from Thorvald Solberg, the Register of Copyrights, to Kerr, Page and Cooper.]

Gentlemen: December 9, 1904
I have the honor, by request of the Librarian of Congress, to acknowledge the receipt of your letter of December 6th in the matter of the application of The American Mutoscope & Biograph Co. for entry of 'The Suburbanite'.

Your letter will be filed with the application

to show the basis upon which action is taken and the entry will be made.

The remittance received from the claimant on November 25th was fifty cents only, which sum is sufficient for entry without certificate, but if the certificate is desired as is intimated in the closing paragraph of your letter, an additional fee of fifty cents would be required. Please see circular 3.

> Respectfully,
> Register of Copyrights.

Inclosure: Circular 3.
Messrs Kerr, Page & Cooper
Singer Building, 149 Broadway
New York, N.Y.

The confusion over whether or not *The Suburbanite* should have been registered in Class A or D was caused at least in part by the actual item deposited with the application form submitted by AM&B. What the AM&B staff sent to the Copyright Office was two copies of the advertising bulletin for *The Suburbanite* (Bulletin no. 37, 28 November 1904) that the company normally produced to advertise its productions for sale to exchangers and theatre owners. The bulletin was a printed document that included a publicity still, the film's length expressed in total number of feet, a listing of each scene in the film, and a detailed description of the action. The Copyright Office's reaction was to interpret the bulletin broadly as a 'book'. However, the intent of the AM&B registration seems to have been to establish the descriptive text contained in bulletin no. 37 as the actual language of Frank J. Marion's original scenario. This conclusion is suggested twice in the text of the Kerr, Page & Cooper letter:

> It is the sole purpose of the composition [the Biograph bulletin copy submitted for registration] that this narrative or story shall be represented dramatically by action, posture and gesture. And, something of novelty may be presented by the fact that this particular dramatic composition [again, the text of *The Suburbanite* bulletin] has been photographed in a series of living pictures, and is susceptible of being represented thereby.

Though the Kerr, Page and Cooper defence won the day for *The Suburbanite*, AM&B seems to have learned from the experience that by registering copies of its advertising bulletins as dramatic compositions, in lieu of actual typescript copies of the original scenarios, they only caused confusion and the added expense to themselves of hiring lawyers. The result was that in the period following the registration of *The Suburbanite*, the next five scenarios registered by AM&B in Class D were accomplished by submitting original typescripts, instead of printed bulletin copies.[4]

Because the original typescript of the Marion scenario for *The Suburbanite* does not exist, it cannot be absolutely proven that the text of bulletin no. 37 was taken directly from it. However, a strong indication that that is the case is contained in the five subsequent AM&B Class D registrations made immediately after *The Suburbanite*, between 17 December 1904 and April 1905, for which copies of original scenario typescripts were deposited for registration and for which the descriptive text exactly matches that used in the corresponding bulletins (numbers 39, 42, 43, 44 and 45). One final note of interest, printed immediately below the title line of *The Suburbanite* bulletin is the prominent notice, 'Copyright 1904, both as a Picture and as a Play, by the American Mutoscope & Biograph Co'. The same notice also appears on the bulletins for *The Wedding*, *The Nihilists*, *The Chicken Thief*, *Tom, Tom the Piper's Son* and *Wanted: A Dog*.[5]

The Serenade (Selig, 1905)

Scenario/Screenplay example no. 2: *The Serenade*, copyrighted on 1 May 1905 (Class D6611) by W.N. Selig.

The next item is a dramatic composition, *The Serenade*, registered by W.N. Selig of 43 Peck Court, Chicago, Illinois, on 1 May 1905; the same W.N. Selig who founded the Selig Polyscope Company in 1896. Because it contains dialogue and instructions for the director and actors, it is truly a recognisable screenplay and is the earliest known document of its kind yet identified. On the title page, this work is described as a 'Dramatic Composition in four scenes'. Page two repeats the credit information and bears the additional notice 'CAUTION – Stage representation, *Moving Pictures*, etc. positively prohibited, without the written consent of the author'. (Italics mine.) The text of *The Serenade* reveals a rather typical farce comedy of the era that well might have been played as either a burlesque stage performance or a split reel comedy. No copy survives in the Library of Congress collection and a search by Zoran Sinobad of the American Film Institute database of major archive holdings around the world reveals no known copies. According to Charles Musser, *The Serenade* was finally produced in a twelve-scene version released by Selig in September 1905.[6] The text as transcribed here preserves the peculiar spelling and punctuation of the original.

The Serenade

Cast of Characters.

> Daddy Skinner (A vicious old man)
> Fannie Skinner (His daughter)
> Freddie Laubert (In love with Fannie)
> Nellie (The Old Mans Bull-dog)
> Ed Hatch (Who owns an Automobile)

The Serenade – Scene One.

Scene: Garden Scene – with balcony projecting from upper part of house. (to left of Stage).

> Enter Freddie, Cornet under his arm stops beneath Balcony, and begins to serenade Fannie, during the serenade, Fannie appears on Balcony.

Freddie: (Stops playing) Ah! my loved one, my own sweet Juliet, come fly with me, to a bower of rose's do not turn me away, but whisper that one dear short but sweet word, that means, all in life to me, say you will this very night, elope with me, and be my wife.

Fannie: Yes I would go with you anywhere, fly with you to the end of the Earth, were it not for my Father.

Old Man: (listening behind Balcony window) Ah! Ha! I see it all now, the Villian, that bargain counter three cent Dude, wants my Daughter to elope with him, Oh! the Scoundrel! the Wretch! I'll fix him.

Freddie: Come with me at once, Darling, we will fly like to birds, to a dear cute little nest, that I'v (sic) prepared for just you and I.

Fannie: Yes Sweetheart, I will I will, oh! how happy

we will be, and such a romantic Marriage, ours will be.

Freddie: This is indeed Heavenly bliss, I'll Serenade you again, my own little Tootsie Wootsie, soon to be my wife, (Begins to play)

> Enter old man on balcony.

Old Man: Fannie, Fannie, I say come in here at once, (to Freddie) you rascal away with you, stop that infernal playing, (to Fannie) as for you march into the house at once, do you hear me?

Fannie: yes Papa, but let me stay, just a minute, (throws a kiss to Freddie)

Old Man: no sir-ee Miss, you march straight into the house, (to Freddie) confound you Sir will you cease that infernal noise, (To Fannie) do you intend to obey your Father or not?

Fannie: but my Freddie, surely you would not harm my Sweetheart?

Old Man: (aside) Oh! No I wont do a single thing to Freddie, I'll only pulverise him thats all (to Freddie) stop that so called music, it's driving me mad. (to Fannie) I command you to instantly enter the house.

Fannie: but supposing that I should refuse, what then?

Old Man: what's this, mutiny in my own house, do I hear right, my Daughter refuse's to obey me, (to Freddie) Oh! you Monster you shall be made to suffer for this. (To Fannie) to think that a Daughter of mine would act this way, go into the house I say, do you hear?

Fannie: yes Father I hear, but for once I must overrule your decision.

Old Man: (to Freddie) Coward! to take advantage of me like this, will you ever stop that alleged music, is it not enough to come here like a mid-night Burglar, and rob me of my most precious possession my Daughter, with-out sending me to an Insane Asylum, with your so-called music. stop it I say, or I shall call the Police.

Fannie: Oh! Father pray dont do any-thing rash, (to Freddie) OH! such Heavenly music, I would that it could go on for ever.

Old Man: not on your life! I'll fix your little Freddie's Clock for him.

Fannie: what would you murder my Freddie, Oh! Father I beseech you, spare his life, do not do him an injury, I love him, and could not see him come to harm.

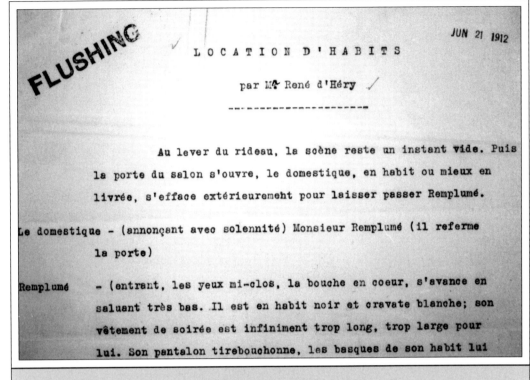

Fig. 2. Top half of the first typescript page for the screenplay of *Location d'habits*, be René d'Héry, copyrighted on 21 June 1912 by the Gaumont Company of Flushing, New York. This document was one of forty such compositions registered by Gaumont in 1912.

Old Man: no he shall be made to suffer as I have, (shakes fist at Freddie)

Fannie: remember you are my Father, and below stand's the only one that has won my heart, Father do not drive him away, or you will break my poor heart. (begins to cry)

Old Man: (aside and shaking his fist at Freddie) I'll break his neck now to get even with him, (to Fannie) no Miss this has gone to far you have made a Demon of me, stand aside I say, it's to late now this has gone too far, I must avenge my outraged feelings, curse him.

(Old man enters house, leaves Fannie on Balcony)

Fannie: (to Freddie) play on my hearts twin, your sweet music has captured my poor lonesome heart, and enraptured my soul.

Old Man: (enters with a bucket of water) now too for-ever rid myself of this Musical absurdity, HA! HA!

Fannie: Great Heavens! Father what would you do?

Old Man: I am going to wash away, all my troubles, look out below I think it's going to rain. (emptys the bucket of water on Freddie, who continues to play un-disturbed)

Fannie: Ah! Father remembers the old saying, 'Love Laughs at Lock-Smiths' beside Freddie don't mind a little thing like water, he used to be a Bell-Diver once.

Old Man: curse him! I am foiled again, but I will win yet, remember, 'He Laughs Best Who Laughs Last'

(Old man rushes into the house frantically tearing his hair, leaving Fannie on Balcony)

Fannie: (leaning over Balcony) Freddie Dear run for your life, I am sure Father will commit a terrible crime, and you will be the victim stop your serenade and fly.

(a loud noise is heard coming from the house. Bull-Dog begins barking. Old man is heard yelling, Sic Em Nellie!)

Freddie: (Begins to play), 'there'll be a Hot Time in the Old Town TO Night'.

Old Man: (enters with Bull-Dog on chain, yelling at the top of his voice), Sic Em! Nellie, chew his leg off. (dog barks furiously and starts for Freddie)

Fannie: Oh! Mercy! look out Freddie, the Dog, he's coming straight for you.

Old Man: no power on Earth can save him now, he's a gone Goose for sure now.

Freddie: (see's Bull-Dog coming, stops playing, and turns to run, but is too late, Bull-Dog with a fierce growl, makes a forward lunge, and grabs Freddie in the seat of the pants, with a life and death grip).

Fannie: all is lost, my poor Freddie will be killed, Oh! father I implore you to call off the dog.

Old Man: never! Ha! Ha! my revenge is complete, I knew I'd get even, and I did. (Fannie faints, Old man stands in door laughing, Freddie is yelling at the top of his voice, Help! Murder! Police! Save me! Bull-Dog clings tenaciously, to Freddies trousers).

(CLOSE IN)

[scenes 2–4 omitted]

Location d'habits (Gaumont, 1912)

Scenario/Screenplay example no. 3: *Location d'habits* by René d'Héry (1912).

The final example of early screenplay writing is a dramatic composition copyrighted by Raymond Gaumont for the Gaumont Company on 21 June 1912. This particular document is one of 41 mostly French-language screenplays registered in June 1912. The clue to its relation to the United States branch of the Gaumont Company is the word 'FLUSHING' stamped on the upper left corner of page one, indicating the location of the Gaumont studios in Flushing, New York. The fact that it is written in French further indicates its connection to the parent company based in France.

LOCATION D'HABITS
par Mr René d'Héry

Au lever du rideau, la scène reste un instant vide. Puis la porte du salon s'ouvre, le domestique, en habit ou mieux en livrée, s'efface extérieurement pour laisser passer Remplumé.

Le domestique: (annonçant avec solennité) Monsieur Remplumé (il referme la porte)

Remplumé: (entrant, les yeux mi-clos, la bouche en coeur, s'avance en saluant très bas. Il est en habit noir et cravate blanche; son vêtement de soirée est infiniment trop long, trop large pour lui. Son pantalon tirebouchonne, les basques de son habit lui tombent sur les talons ; il semble qu'il a revêtu le costume d'un autre deux fois plus large et plus grand que lui. Donc, il entre avec componction et va saluer très bas, un fauteuil vide) (Son salut fini, il se redresse et s'aperçoit que le fauteuil devant lequel il se prosterne n'est pas occupé. Son regard fait le tour de la scène) Personne!.... J'arrive trop tôt. Tant mieux, ce moment de répit me permettra de me remettre.

(Il prononce Ma'me la Comtesse. Il tient son chapeau haut de forme à la main. Quand il a fini sa tirade, il s'oublie à le remettre sur sa tête. Mais ce chapeau haut de forme est tout le contraire de son habit, il est infiniment trop étroit. Reprenant son chapeau à la main.) Il est un peu étroit. (il considère son chapeau) Beaucoup trop étroit même. Dame! On fait ce qu'on peut: Je suis venu à Paris en veston et en casquette: de sorte que pour me présenter devant Madame la Comtesse de Haussecolles j'ai dûlouer ce chapeau et l'habit que je porte, au Temple. Le chapeau est vraiment trop étroit, il n'y a pas à dire (se carrant dans son costume) Mais l'habit me va, oh! là, tout à fait. La loueuse m'a dit, 'Y vous va comme un gant' (Se promenant dans son habit satisfait) (Il aperçoit une glace au-dessus de la cheminé. Il s'en approche pour voir l'effet de son costume, mais ne se reconnaissant pas, il se retourne croyant qu'il a derrière lui quelqu'un que la glace lui renvoie. Mais non, il n'y a pas d' erreur. C'est bien lui) Comment, c'est moi! ... Ah! Bien je comprends que je sois à mon aise là-dedans! ... (il se regarde, voit son pantalon; il plie les genoux et les basques de son vêtement touchant à terre) Je ne veux pas être ridicule (subitement résolu) Filons! (il va à la porte)

(Au moment où il va ouvrir la porte, la porte s'ouvre, le domestique apparait dans l'encadrement et annonce:)

Le domestique: Monsieur Lapalette.

(Remplumé s'est sauvé à travers le salon et a été se tapir, tout mince, tout ratatiné dans un coin; il rentrerait sous terre s'il le pouvait.)

(Lapalette entre. Il est vêtu identiquement comme Remplumé, avec cette différence notable cependant, que tout, pantalon, gilet et habit lui sont infiniment trop étroits et trop courts. Les manches lui découvrent les poignets jusqu'aux avant-bras, et le pantalon montre ses chaussettes jusqu'au dessus des chevilles, Seul le chapeau haut de forme quand il le mettra sur sa tête, tout à l'heure lui descendra jusqu'aux yeux.

Lapaltette: (après un regard circulaire) Personne. Tant mieux. (il regarde le salon) Ah! bien si moi Lapalette, garçon de bureau, j'avais jamais pu prévoir que je serais reçu chez une noble comtesse du faubourg! Ce matin le patron m'a dit: 'Lapalette veux-tu aller au théâtre? – v'láune place. Je garde son billet (il tire le billet de sa poche et lit) 'La Comtesse de Haussecolles prie M. Miroteau de … etc.' 'On fera de la musique et on jouera la comédie.' Alors, comme je n'ai pas de vêtement de soirée, j'ai loué celui-ci au Temple. Y me va comme un gant m'a dit la loueuse. Le faiat est qu'il me moule positivement … Il n'y a que le chapeau (il le met) Un peu large, ça m'évitera la migraine. (Pendant qu'il parle Remplumé, en tapinois est sorti de son coin et, se glissant contre le mur, a gagné la porte. Il se trouve nez à nez avec Lapalette qui sort aussi.)

Lapalette: (a part) Oh! Un invité (il salue) (haut) Pardon, monsieur, je me trouve bien chez la Comtesse de … (il aperçoit le costume démesuré de Remplumé et il éclate de rire) Ah! Ah! Ah! Elle est bien bonne. Ah! Ah! Ah!

Remplumé: (L'imitant) (furieux) Ah!Ah!Ah! Vous trouvez çà drôle?

Lapalette: ?

Remplumé: De vous mettre en accordéon pour me parler?

Lapalette: (vexé) A moins qu'on le fasse exprès pour faire pouffer les gens, on ne sort pas dans une tenue pareille.

Remplumé: (ironique) Veuillez donc jeter un regard dans cette glace.

Lapalette: (après s'être regardé dans la glace au-dessus de la cheminée) Est-ce bien moi?

Lapalette: Comme un gant, qu'elle a dit, comme un gant.

Remplumé: Identique! Où vous êtes-vous fait habiller?

Lapalette: Au Temple.

Remplumé: Moi aussi.

Lapalette: Tout le théatre va se moquer de nous!

Remplumé: Comment! elle a un théatre?

Lapalette: Oui, voyon? Qu'est-ce que vous venez donc faire, si ce n'est assister à la comédie?

Remplumé: Voici pourquoi je viens. Faut vous dire que j'exerce la profession de grainetier à Suzy les Tripettes où Madame le Comtesse a son château. Cet été, Madame la Comtesse, à qui j'avais été livrer du grain, daigna me dire: 'Monsieur Remplumé, si vous veniez à Paris, ne manquez pas de venir me voir. Je suis venu à Paris pour visiter l'exposition agricole et me voici.'

Lapalette: De sorte que vous ne vous doutiez pas du tout que vous assisteriez tout à l'heure au spectacle?

Remplumé: Pas du tout … Mais, êtes-vous bien sur …

Lapalette: Voice le billet de faveur que mon patron m'a donné (il montre son billet)

Remplumé: (éclatant de rire) Hi! Hi! Hi! Mais c'est une invitation, à une réception que vous me montrez là! Votre patron s'est trompé de papier! Hi! Hi! Hi!

Lapalette: Me voilà bien.

Remplumé: Vous voilà mal habillé que vous voulez dire! Il est vrai que je ne le suis pas mieux que vous.

Lapalette: (se frappant le front) Oh! une idée … Peut être que le constume de l'un irait à l'autre? Troquons-les!

Allons oust!

Remplumé: Oui, vite, vite …

(Ils retirent leur habit, leur gilet qu'ils jettent pêle-même à terre. Au moment, la porte s'ouvre. Le domestique apparait dans l'encadrement et annonce ave sonnité:)

Le domestique - Madame la Comtesse de Haussecolles …

(Remplumé et Lapalettes se jettent avec furie sur leurs vêtements pour les reprendre pendant que le rideau et que les invités paraissent au fond.)♠

Notes

1. The classification system continued to be expanded in later years. Because the technology of motion pictures was based on common principles of photomechanical technology, they were registered from 1901 on as 'photographs' in Classes H and later J, until 28 August 1912, when two separate classes (L and M) were created especially for motion pictures

– Class L for fictional films (photoplays) and Class M for non-fiction and animation films.

2. Frank J. Marion soon after became one of the founders of the Kalem Company. In 1907 Kalem itself became famous in the legal history of motion picture screenwriting when it was sued by Harper Brothers, the original publishers of Lew Wallace's *Ben Hur*, for adapting the novel to motion pictures without permission. The case was eventually decided against Kalem in 1911 by the United States Supreme Court, with the majority decision written by Oliver Wendell Holmes.

3. The word 'apparently' was inserted by hand between the lines of the typewritten letter, probably by Solberg.

4. The following five works were copyrighted by AM&B as motion pictures (Class H) and scenarios (Class D) during a period immediately after *The Suburbanite* was registered on 25 November 1904: *The Chicken Thief* (17 December 1904; D5917), *Tom, Tom the Piper's Son* (6 March 1905; D6287), *The Nihilists* (20 March 1905; D6365), *The Wedding* (20 March 1905; D6700) and *Wanted A Dog* (12 April 1905; D6532).

5. For reproductions of relevant AM&B bulletins before 1908, see: Kemp Niver, ed., *Biograph Bulletins, 1896–1908*, (Los Angeles: Locare Research Group, 1971). For information on Biograph bulletins after 1908 see: Eileen Bowser, ed., *Biograph Bulletins, 1908 to 1912* (New York: Octagon Books, 1973).

6. Charles Musser, *The Emergence of Cinema: The American Screen to 1907* (New York: Charles Scribner's Sons, 1990), 400.

Film History, Volume 9, pp. 300–319, 1997. Copyright © John Libbey & Company
ISSN: 0892-2160. Printed in Australia

'Have you the power?' The Palmer Photoplay Corporation and the film viewer/author in the 1920s

Anne Morey

In *Babbitt* (1922), Sinclair Lewis provides his readers with the full text of an advertisement for a correspondence course in public speaking that has caught young Ted Babbitt's eye, and which he hopes to convince his father to allow him to sign up for in place of the more conventional college education. The language of this advertisement, with its emphasis on 'personality' and its enthusiasm for power over other people, suggests that education is developing a new instrumentality in the 1920s. As *Babbitt's* narrator notes, 'above the picture [of a young man holding an audience of middle-aged men rapt] was an inspiring educational symbol – no antiquated lamp or torch or owl of Minerva, but a row of dollar signs'.[1]

While the courses that appeal to Ted range from oratory to boxing, correspondence schools sought to provide expertise in other fields as well. In particular, during the 1910s and 1920s, a number of such schools promised to prepare men and women for jobs in the film industry, especially as screenwriters. The Palmer Photoplay Corporation in Los Angeles (founded in 1918) was perhaps the largest and most successful of these outfits, although others flourished in large and small cities across the

nation.[2] Cynically viewed, these schools might appear only to be in the business of separating customers from their money, since the freelance market for manuscripts collapsed in the late 1910s, and the likelihood of a private individual's placing a screenplay with a studio was small.[3] The thriving nature of Palmer Photoplay's business as late as the mid-1920s (when it began to shift its attention to instruction in short story writing and general self-expression) suggests, however, that achieving material success in Hollywood may not have been the sole motive for subscribers, or indeed for the school's management.

Palmer located itself at the crossroads of a

Anne Morey is a Ph.D. candidate in the Radio-Television-Film Department at the University of Texas at Austin, and is completing a dissertation on the rhetorics used to encourage and control outsider participation in the film industry during the silent and early sound periods. She has published in *The Spectator* and in *Tulsa Studies in Women's Literature*, among other venues. Correspondence to: RTF Dept., CMA 6.118, UT-Austin, Austin, TX 78712,USA or e-mail: moreyam@mail.utexas.edu.

number of contradictory rhetorics about the nature and destiny of the American film industry during the early 1920s. These rhetorics, as we shall see, sort themselves out along a number of axes – democratic/elitist, individual/corporate, private/public, original/hackneyed. While fashioning more and better screenwriters was the avowed purpose of this school, its inability to guarantee material success obliged it to present other motivations for subscribing to its customers. Its expressed aims ranged from the fostering of a sense of kinship between audience and producer to addressing defects in 'personality' and general education. Beyond these overt motivations, however, lay the less frequently expressed desire to create a 'better' audience – more engaged, more informed, more invested in Hollywood; in short, an audience sympathetic to (because knowledgeable about) the industry and the medium. In a slippage that now seems characteristic of the 1910s and 1920s, we find that it is not things or products that are being mass-produced but people. Henry Ford asserted that he manufactured men (through the Americanisation of his workers) rather than motor cars. The Palmer Photoplay Corporation manufactured superior audience members rather than screenwriters *tout court*.

To this end, the school worked to promote a notion of self-expression that was simultaneously standardised and individual. In a number of approaches potentially working toward a kind of Taylorisation of self-expression, student work was to be presented to potential buyers in a uniform format, the school's stock in trade was instruction in 'technique', and students were advised as a group to avoid certain topics (costume plays, war and Bible pictures) and stylistic fillips (reliance on melodrama and coincidence, for example). Indeed, the standardisation of Palmer students began with a psychological questionnaire designed to divine talent for photoplaywriting, which all students were required to submit with their applications. At the same time, however, the school necessarily preached the gospel of individual success through self-fashioning, the importance of originality, and the evils of the Eastern publishing establishment and industry reliance on adaptation.

These competing rhetorics do not arise merely from Palmer's advertising, nor do they result simply

from its rather quixotic mission of preparing students for a freelance screenplay market that had largely disappeared by the time the school was founded. Rather, the rhetorical contradictions manifested by the school's materials are likewise to be found in trade paper and general circulation periodical articles discussing the nature and destiny of the film industry. The place of the 'pre-sold' film property, the question of the desirability or undesirability of adaptation, and concerns over the intellectual development of audiences and the place of film in American culture became focuses of public debate in a wide variety of venues during the early 1920s. As a particular node within the nexus of these debates over the social role of the film industry, the Palmer Corporation deserves examination because it was in Hollywood but not exactly of it. Many of its personnel had connections to studios, and its advisory council boasted such luminaries as Cecil B. DeMille, Lois Weber and Thomas Ince. While Palmer engaged in film manufacture briefly in 1924, it was not a studio within the conventional understanding of that term. Rather, Palmer offered itself as a liaison between Hollywood and the American public, addressing its students primarily as would-be members of the industry.

* * *

Palmer offered remarkably comprehensive services. While many competing 'correspondence' schools simply offered a single book sent in exchange for a couple of dollars, the Palmer course was designed to take a year, although the term could be extended. During the enrolment period, subscribers received several books (among them the *Photoplay Plot Encyclopedia*, described as 'an analysis of the use in photoplays of the thirty-six dramatic situations and their subdivisions'), twelve lectures, and a newsletter reviewing current releases, as well as a monthly magazine, *Photodramatist*, giving advice on scenario writing and observations on the current state of Hollywood.[4] In addition to the manuals, the organisation also provided exercises to work through and a revision and placement service for manuscripts. Subscription rates ranged from $55 to $75 in the 1910s and from $76.50 to $90 in the 1920s, depending upon which plan students took.[5] As part of their original investment, students were entitled to send in five manuscripts to be critiqued; the placement depart-

FREDERICK PALMER

Fig. 1. Frederick Palmer, President of the Palmer Photoplay Corporation. [Photo courtesy of Richard Koszarski].

ment would undertake to sell acceptable manuscripts for a ten per cent commission. Moreover, in the summer of 1922, the corporation began producing films, known (of course) as Palmerplays.

In presenting this wealth of materials, early Palmer advertisements employed rhetorical devices nearly identical to those of Lewis's fictional example, quoted at the beginning of this article. An advertisement in *Photoplay* elects the 'power over others' motif, with a headline that inquires, 'Who told Chas. Ray [an actor providing a testimonial for the corporation] to act this way?'[6] Other ads em-

phasised the monetary benefits of the Palmer Plan ('not a mere book nor a "school", nor a tedious correspondence course'), suggesting that one might make between $100 and $1000 from a properly presented photoplay idea. They also routinely emphasised the dearth of original ideas, in effect identifying the artistic vacuum into which the amateur might step.[7]

Later advertisements suggest that the corporation's focus was shifting from scenario writing to more general literary pursuits by 1925, inasmuch as the coupon lists photoplaywriting as only one option among others, including short story writing, English expression, and business letter writing.[8] This shift in focus is not surprising, given that the freelance market for photoplays appears to have diminished by 1916.[9] The possibilities represented by such a market, however, were kept alive by fan magazines into the 1920s, through a variety of types of articles. Some of these pieces were nonfiction, such as the 1919 series signed by Anita Loos and John Emerson offering practical advice on photoplaywriting; others were fictional treatments of the circumstances of freelance writers, such as Frederick Arnold Kummer's 'The Rejected One' (1918), the story of a young man who repeatedly tries to sell his work to a studio and finally gets past the Cerberus at the scenario editor's desk by putting his work inside a cover with a well-known author's name on it. Although this saga is cast as fiction, the hero's strategy, as we shall see, is not unlike that offered by Palmer to its unknown students.[10]

The possibility of amateur or outsider participation in the film industry was also kept alive into the 1920s through the promotion of screenwriting contests. For a time in the early and mid-1910s, there may indeed have been a dearth of stories available for filming. Edward Azlant suggests that the 1911 Supreme Court ruling that found literary properties to be tangible goods (and consequently protected from unauthorised adaptation) resulted in the increased solicitation of story material from all sources, including the general public.[11] Certainly throughout the 1910s and into the 1920s contests for screenplays and screenplay ideas were common. As early as 1916, however, a trade paper commentator labelled such contests mere advertising stunts (and not the entree into a career they were sometimes represented as being), but they remained a prominent way of soliciting public participation in Hollywood's destiny.[12]

The scenario contest offered the means for the 'discovery' of a new talent as late as 1922, a phenomenon that Palmer advertising capitalised upon. Contests especially fostered the double rhetoric of film as a democratic enterprise that nonetheless offered the potential for individual elevation above the common herd. In April 1922, Goldwyn Pictures and the Chicago *Daily News* jointly solicited manuscripts in a contest whose top prize was $10,000; it attracted 27,000 submissions.[13] Winifred Kimball's 'Broken Chains' won first place, and she was claimed as a Palmer graduate in a July 1922 *Photodramatist* advertisement that observed that 'more than $20,000 of the $40,000 offered in prizes during the last year or so has been won by Palmer students'.[14]

Even in the absence of a reliable freelance market, then, the Palmer Plan still represented a good investment if one were fortunate enough to win a contest. The celebrity associated with winning a contest may have led, however, to a confusion between person and product. For example, in what one finds to be a persistent blurring of the divide between self and commodity, Kimball's personal narrative of success is conflated with the narrative sold to be made into a film:

> These three years [of Kimball's apprenticeship with Palmer] were no easy period of casual study. To have the dark tragedy of suicide twice enter one's home, to be forced into reduced circumstances with others dependent on one for support, to have the high faith and courage to spend money and time from a slender store on the study of dramatic art, to persist gamely through three years of discouragement while things grew steadily worse and the mortgage on the old home became past due ... It is a narrative of fact with a dramatic climax only equalled by her photoplay story 'Broken Chains'.[15]

In fact, in this account, it is hard to say whether the study of technique or the endurance of hardship had more to do with the success of Kimball's work. The blurring of boundaries between individual and marketable script, however, suggest that this rhetoric furthers a fairly concerted promotion of the project of self-commodification.

Palmer students were urged to think of themselves as simultaneously the raw material for their potential success and the agents acting upon this raw material. The course itself was the sympathetic and knowledgeable guide that would enable the student 'to profit from the undeveloped resources of [his] own imagination'.[16] Self-commodification through the mastery of screenwriting technique offers the possibility of reconciling some of the instabilities latent in the opposition between creative individual and standardising system. As Walter

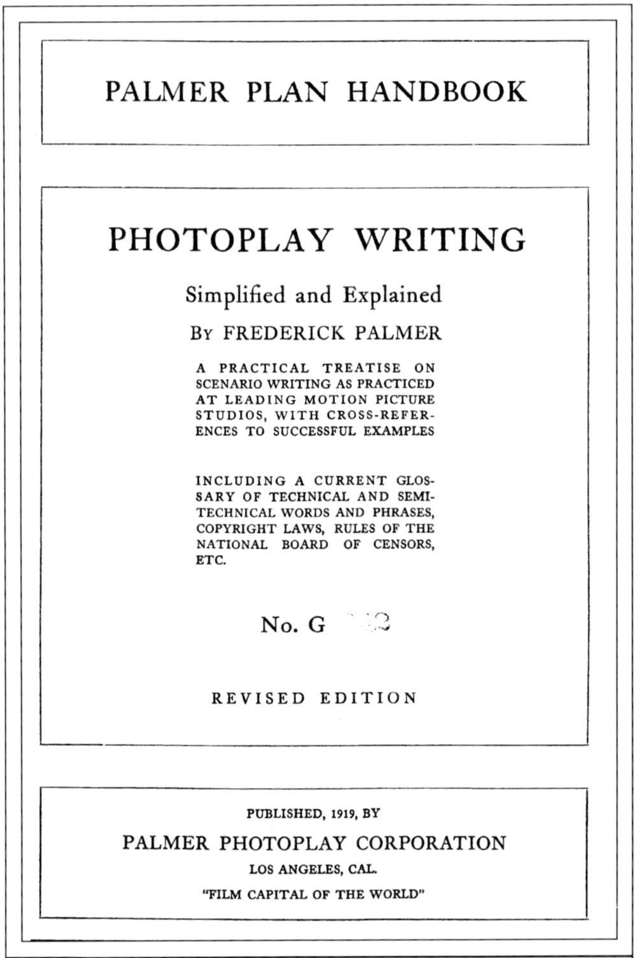

Benn Michaels has argued in the context of Progressive Era literature, 'individuality now appears as an effect of standardisation'.[17] The quality of being somebody, namely an individual, emerges through the adoption of methods designed, ironically, to apply to anyone who wishes for success. In the case of Palmer, in other words, slavish attention to one-size-fits-all instruction will ultimately result in success designed to lift one above the common herd.

The Palmer advertising literature suggests that the development of self-expression, self-mastery, and, above all, 'personality' was every bit as rewarding and significant as was the prospect of becoming the next C. Gardner Sullivan, whose salary was listed as $104,000 in one Palmer brochure.[18] By fostering the development of self-expression, the Palmer Plan offers a new self, as Roy Manker, the Corporation's vice-president, points out:

> The highest achievement of mankind is not a million dollars, but a personality. The ability to see and tell a story contributes immensely towards the formation of personality ... It is a realisation of this that is awakening more people to the value of knowing how to talk and write well, than ever gave the subject a thought in the past. The printing press is partly responsible. The drawing together of people into cities and close daily contact is just as responsible. Every one wants to be set off a little in the crowd, and he recognises that the readiest means to that end is the practice of the short story teller's art.[19]

This emphasis on the formation of personality implies that the Palmer Plan is best viewed within the context of the larger culture of personality that operated, according to Warren Susman, from the late nineteenth century onward. According to Susman's analysis of the terms associated with personality printed in advice manuals of the 1880s through

---

PALMER PLAN HANDBOOK

PHOTOPLAY WRITING

Simplified and Explained

By FREDERICK PALMER

A PRACTICAL TREATISE ON
SCENARIO WRITING AS PRACTICED
AT LEADING MOTION PICTURE
STUDIOS, WITH CROSS-REFER-
ENCES TO SUCCESSFUL EXAMPLES

INCLUDING A CURRENT GLOS-
SARY OF TECHNICAL AND SEMI-
TECHNICAL WORDS AND PHRASES,
COPYRIGHT LAWS, RULES OF THE
NATIONAL BOARD OF CENSORS,
ETC.

No. G

REVISED EDITION

PUBLISHED, 1919, BY
PALMER PHOTOPLAY CORPORATION
LOS ANGELES, CAL.
"FILM CAPITAL OF THE WORLD"

Fig. 2. Title page of the *Palmer Plan Handbook* [courtesy of John Belton].

---

the 1920s, the culture of personality emphasised the 'masterful, creative, dominant, forceful'.[20] Those who had personality could stand out from the crowd, being different while at the same time appealing to the crowd. To return to Michaels's insight, then, individuality results from standardisation because mastery results from meeting standards, and the individual within the culture of personality is above all masterful.

The mastery that the Palmer course offered rests upon the absorption of 'technique', which is represented as a discrete body of knowledge, the possession of which separates the tyro from the adept. In some instances, technical mastery is described as a new form of linguistic competence, which may range from learning the vocabulary of filmmaking to beginning to think in a new, more visual language. As Frederick Palmer observes of his own development as a writer after he achieved a new understanding of photoplay construction, 'not only did I immediately begin to see a new light, but I really began to think in a *new language*'.[21] New linguistic competence aside, however, students were advised to eschew the very vocabulary they were picking up from the Palmer Plan: 'Do not attempt to use the technical terms contained in the Glossary when preparing a synopsis for submission. Tell your story in clear, simple language.'[22]

By and large, the information that the course imparted was useful, inasmuch as it reflected established Hollywood practice.[23] In less elaborate form, however, much of the information was also available in trade papers, books, and fan magazines, reflecting the widespread interest in screenwriting during this period. Among the pieces of advice offered to students were pointers on how to prepare manuscripts and where to send them; *Photodramatist* included a regular column on the state of the market). Additionally, the various lectures and manuals emphasised the importance of action (in place of the more novelistic description or 'philosophy'), ways of developing profitable characterisation, and methods of structuring suspenseful plots.[24] Many of the instructional materials underlined the visual nature of film; among the more arcane assignments is a prolonged exercise in 'visualisation', in which the student is to imagine a room in detail, people it, and then place these imaginary figures in conflict with each other. Even this assignment is an opportunity for the exercise of mastery: 'Start visualising in a passive mood ... Then resume control. Become master of your visualisation, bringing logic and reason into action ... in a short time you will experience the magic of becoming a monarch of the limitless domain of your own imagination.'[25]

The design of the course navigated the shoals of conflicting representations of authorial success. Success was the product both of labour (a democratic conceit) and of talent (a more elitist conceit). The Corporation thus chose to represent success as the result of latent ability rigorously developed. In this way, it restored what was ostensibly missing from the new culture of personality – equality of

opportunity within an industry that otherwise might appear exclusive because of its privileging of looks, talent, or hard-to-obtain experience. If the rhetoric of Hollywood has provoked admiration for and envy of the chosen few, other rhetorics defuse any potential unhappiness that might result from this strategy.

In this respect, screenwriting appeared to have a privileged position as a safe means of ascent. While acting, too, was a subject ostensibly taught by correspondence schools, such instruction always looked shadier than the similar instruction offered by Palmer and its competitors. A *Photoplay* article contemporary with the first Palmer advertisement exposed the risks of being fleeced by a Los Angeles school of acting, and by late 1923 the MPPDA promised to crack down on three abuses of the motion picture industry: fraudulent schools of acting (both correspondence and otherwise), fraudulent stock schemes, and fraudulent scenario writing schools.[26] Whereas acting schools were serious objects of concern because they appeared to induce young women (in particular) to leave their homes for distinctly unlikely career prospects, writing could be done at home, and unlike acting seemed to validate the part that more conventional forms of education might play in success. Screenwriting, then, promised to allow the creation of a new self in a way that need not threaten the old order.

To be sure, there was at least one critic who found what the Palmer Plan had to offer rather unsavoury by 1924. Epes Winthrop Sargent, author of a 1913 photoplaywriting book entitled *Technique of the Photoplay*, wrote a stinging account of an unnamed correspondence school in Los Angeles, probably Palmer.[27] Credulous students, Sargent complains, are induced to give up safe if boring positions elsewhere and move to Los Angeles to be near the action. Sargent taxes the errant school with holding out bait such as film production schemes (Palmer began producing Palmerplays in 1922) in order to keep up subscriptions even after a wide variety of periodicals, addressing both the trade and the general reader, had trumpeted the collapse of the freelance market.[28]

Presumably, students' continued enrolment in such courses during the early 1920s was at least partly the result of the rhetoric that Hollywood itself

"TOO STUPID"

Knut Hamsun came over from Norway some years ago and got a job washing dishes in a restaurant. He was "fired." His employer told him he was "too stupid" to wash dishes. Maybe he was. Knut got a job on a Chicago street car. The superintendent "fired" him. He couldn't remember the names of the streets. "Too stupid," was the verdict.

Successively Knut became porter in a hotel, coal passer on a steamship, deckhand, and many other things. Always he was discharged and usually the boss told him he was too stupid to "earn his salt."

But Knut wasn't too stupid to write fifteen volumes of poems, which have been translated into seventeen languages, and which have delighted readers the world over. He wasn't too stupid to write novels no one can forget after reading. He wasn't too stupid to earn and receive the Nobel prize for literature, nearly $50,000. He wasn't too stupid to become one of the world's really great writers.

Yet he was a failure as a dishwasher.

On the other hand, many a failure in literature would make a fine street-car conductor.—Editorial, Los Angeles Record.

WHO KNOWS BUT WHAT *YOU* ARE ANOTHER KNUT HAMSUN?

It is said that Marshall Neilan, the famous director, was a taxicab driver, and that C. Gardner Sullivan, Ince's $100,000 a year scenario writer, was a farmer boy. People get to be famous in the motion picture business in just a short while. The purpose of the League is to give you YOUR OPPORTUNITY.

PHOTOPLAYWRIGHTS LEAGUE OF AMERICA

621-7 Union League Building   Los Angeles, Calif.

Fig. 3. A little story of success from a company in competition with the Palmer Plan, the Photoplaywrights League of America [courtesy of Richard Koszarski].

was using about film's destiny as an art form. The 'original' story, one that was neither an adaptation nor hackneyed, was held out as the ideal to which the industry must ultimately adhere. That many commentators discussed the dearth of original material may have suggested to the attentive film 'outsider', fan, or would-be author that there was in fact an opening for him or her, despite other an-

nouncements to the contrary. Similarly, journals such as the *Film Spectator* called for instruction in the arts associated with the film industry, suggesting a vast arena of technical knowledge not yet possessed by many, an argument that may have promoted the notion that this relatively young field was not yet overcrowded.[29] To some, the presentation of scenario writing as a technical rather than a literary subject may have made it particularly appealing because it was the more modern, and perhaps the more teachable. Correspondence schools in other subjects, such as bookkeeping and engineering, had already established interest in opportunities of acquiring knowledge with an immediate market value, or, alternatively, putting to practical use culture already acquired.

Here again the correspondence school profited from a remarkable double-edged rhetoric; Hollywood was represented both as the means of escape from office drudgery and as a work environment very like the one that Palmer students evidently wished to avoid. In a Palmer pamphlet offering the potential customer *Little Stories of Success*, people whose present work was unfulfilling were precisely those solicited:

> Why pour your energies into a task that is distasteful, when by using a part of your spare time you may prepare for a position worthy of your ability? Why remain at an inferior station and watch the rest of the world enjoy advantages and possessions that you too may share? Why strain your energies to make adequate a mediocre income when you may have the equal of your present whole year's salary in one successful photoplay?[30]

The Palmer literature acknowledges, however, the alteration in the structure of the freelance market by suggesting employment in 'high salaried positions as staff scenarists' as an alternative (or addition) to the achievement of 'large incomes as free-lance writers'.[31] Four of the twenty-four fortunate writers profiled in the pamphlet – two men and two women – were members of some studio's staff.[32] That fourteen of the writers listed were women suggests that women were as eager as men were to escape the rut of office, department store, or home in order to pursue careers as 'freelances' or as members of the staff of a studio.[33]

Thus Palmer's promise of employment in the film industry represents the possibility of escape from the Taylorised labour of other work environments (including the home, which during the 1910s and 1920s was fast becoming another Taylorised zone). At the same time, it is itself Taylorised in that it promotes the Taylorisation of self-expression. Success as a photoplaywright offered a possible solution to the somewhat troubled opposition of individual and crowd, inasmuch as it would lift one above the herd not only financially but also through the acquisition of verbal mastery. But in order to achieve that success, the Palmer literature argued, one had to join another crowd of like-minded people. In fact, only by joining the ranks of Palmer students could one be assured of a fair shake in the battle to enter the film industry. Not only would one learn what the Palmer Plan had to teach (which, presumably, would have the effect of standardising to some degree the output of all students who followed it), but one would benefit at the same time from the features of the Plan especially designed to secure acceptance of one's work.

Precisely because the Plan was the artifact of a fairly sizeable corporate undertaking, it could offer students the 'personal' touch. The sales department, headed by Kate Corbaley, herself the quondam winner of a photoplay contest,[34] affords an ideal example of the numerous ways in which Palmer was able to present itself as a corporate enterprise working in the interests of specific individuals. The department offered its services as agent for qualified students. It was also available in that role to professional writers willing to pay a $25 annual subscription. It advertised that it kept its fingers on the pulse of the business by performing the scientific study of market conditions that most students would not have been able to do for themselves. Scripts were often submitted with specific actors in mind, so the author needed to know where particular stars might be working and what kind of stories interested them. Corbaley observes:

> It is quite impossible for authors living at a distance to keep a record of these changes [in employment or desired subject matter], for by the time they are reported in the trade publications a week or a month may have elapsed and still another change may have been made ... It is the business of the Palmer Sales Department to keep in daily contact with these fluctuating activities and maintain an accurate record of all changes that occur.[35]

The personal touch available within the confines of a large corporation also arises from the sales techniques that Palmer uses: stories 'are not mailed promiscuously to one studio, and then, if rejected, to another', but rather hand-carried by a Palmer representative and discussed with a scenario editor, producer, director or star.[36]

In its guise as agent, the sales department enforced uniformity of appearance for every manuscript sent out for consideration. The process, as Corbaley describes it, was designed partly to give each story polish and partly to discourage plagiarism on the part of unscrupulous studios:

> Stories passed upon favorably by the Sales Department are sent to the typing room to be copied on our special manuscript paper. This paper is steel gray and each page is outlined in blue lines; the typing is done in blue ink of the same color as the ruling and each page carries at the bottom in small blue letters the name, Palmer Photoplay Corporation. These pages are placed in a rough gray folder, bound into book form, the cover bearing the print of the seal of the Corporation in blue and red ... Thus the Palmer Photoplay Corporation presents the scenario-synopsis in conjunction with the author.[37]

This treatment of the salable submission in effect mass-produces manuscripts. Agented, retyped, protected from plagiarism through its association with the corporation (which registers each scenario it submits to studios), the student's idea has become physical artefact, commodity, and part of a national brand,[38] so that it is enabled to achieve success on its merits, much as the hero of Kummer's story discovers that tucking his scenario inside a folder bearing a well-known name will get the manuscript the entree denied it heretofore. Moreover, in keeping with other corporations developing national brands, Palmer unites a dispersed workforce into a single production operation, extolling its instruction department as 'a necessary adjunct or "feeder" for the sales department, to which it looks for its chief source of revenue in the future'.[39]

Significantly, the sales function is reserved for the corporation, and the student is discouraged from taking it up: 'The author must be well equipped with knowledge of photoplay plot technique, but it is equally necessary that the selling agent base his

efforts on a market technique that may be learned only after intensive experience and a definite study of the many angles and details of selling'.[40] At this point, the successful student is producing wealth for himself and for the corporation, which takes a ten per cent commission on any sales gained through its sales department. The student is not permitted to forget that motion pictures are a collaborative art and that his achievement is therefore dependent to some extent on the assistance of others, as *The Essentials of Photoplay Writing* points out: 'When you submit a photoplay synopsis you have the assistance of staff scenario writers, directors, actors, scenery and expert photography to amplify all the little details of production'.[41]

Collaboration also appears in other spheres of photoplay labour. If students finds it too disheartening to work alone until success arrives, they can read the advertisements suggesting collaborative endeavours in their monthly *Photodramatist*. Beyond that, they can join one of the many groups of Palmer students springing up around the country. At first, these groups were greeted as an excellent idea in *Photodramatist*, when David Bader (a student) wrote in to thank Frederick Palmer for his offer of help in setting up such a club. Their program was to read a chapter of the Palmer Plan, discuss it, and then analyse recent films.[42] Apparently, meetings at such clubs could become counterproductive or lead to acrimonious argument. The *Photodramatist* counselled against them three months later, arguing that working alone resulted in greater originality. Given that the construction of a new self is no easy task, what was even worse than the spread of technical errors through the absorption of misconceptions disseminated by one's fellow students was the communication of despair:

> In one Palmer Club that disbanded the disintegration process started when the vibrations of one hapless little discourager began filtering around. Almost every member of the club submitted at least one manuscript to the Palmer revision department. Every one was returned. One or two gloomy mortals did the rest, and almost every member of the 'club' began to believe that he or she lacked any talent, that the future was hopeless.[43]

While students might do well to study together,

it was clearly not in Palmer's best interests to promote comparing notes about relative abilities or rates of success.

Indeed, on the same principle, Palmer had to urge already enrolled students not to fill out the questionnaire used to divine the talent and readiness of the not-yet-enrolled. The rhetoric of the brochures walked a fine line between inclusiveness (anyone can learn to write photoplays if properly taught) and exclusiveness (only those with some native ability, even if presently obscure, can follow the Plan to success). Partly this rhetoric was shaped by the exigencies of the business, which could not safely appear to be encouraging the hopeless simply to extort more money from them. Just as importantly, however, this rhetoric resulted from the same uneasy relation between individual and crowd that produced some fraction of the audience for correspondence schools in the first place – the desire to distinguish oneself while remaining in touch with those one hoped to impress or dominate. The crowd of which one was a member had, at least, to be an elite crowd, and as such, it would appear that Palmer students had to be reminded at intervals that they wrote for the entertainment of the masses, not for an audience of a select few.[44]

It is interesting to contemplate such (unreliable) membership figures as are presently available in light of this tension between classes and masses, elite author and more plebeian audience.[45] Palmer invited current members to sign up family and friends, thus encouraging enrolment, which certainly suggests inclusiveness.[46] At the same time, however, the corporation was at pains to suggest that many more potential students were weeded out by the admission questionnaire than were in fact permitted to enrol. *Photodramatist* reported in 1922 that:

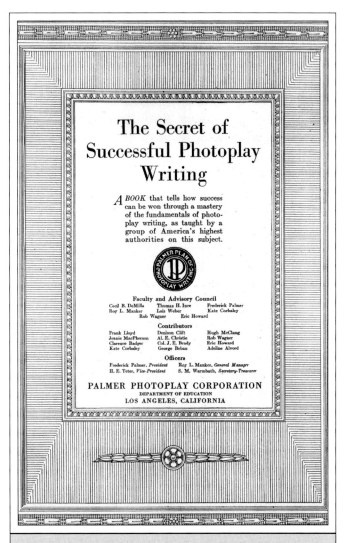

Fig. 4. Palmer's Advisory Council included Cecil B. DeMille, Thomas H. Ince, Lois Weber, Rob Wagner and others [courtesy of Richard Koszarski].

... in this year, between January and 1 July, 4301 of the people who applied to the Palmer Photoplay Corporation for the psychological test which serves as their entrance examination, were rejected. Out of every 100 applicants, only 12 are invited to enroll and only three out of 12, – in other words, three out of the 100 – pass with distinction. The other nine are told they can take the course on their own responsibility and are warned that the way will be hard.[47]

Similarly, *Moving Picture World* listed among Frederick Palmer's successes the fact that he had 'turned down close to 50,000 applicants' in less than five years.[48]

Nonetheless, in 1921 Palmer framed his mission in terms of the mass-production of manuscripts, needed to fill the demand for acceptable stories:

> Gradually the realization came to me that there lay before me a mission in life that might be more useful and more far-reaching than the writing of photoplays; for if I could reach and teach others to do what I was doing I could indirectly be the cause of producing a far greater supply of manuscripts than any single writer or limited group of writers could ever hope to do.[49]

Palmer is frequently described as having written 52 scenarios in nine months, so that he is entitled to speak of screenwriting as a form of industrial production (although his record was established around 1910–11 when scenarios were substantially shorter and less complicated).[50] As he delicately notes, he is the indirect cause of more manuscripts, but this passage glosses over the most important industrial production the school engages in: the manufacture of the students who write those manuscripts.

The enrolment figures, which we may take with a grain of salt, are offered at just the moment (Fall 1922) that Palmer is expanding into film production, which represents the crowning moment of collaboration and, incidentally, further vertical integration on the part of the corporation. Now the school will instruct its students *and* critique, agent, and produce their works. Because Palmer has many mansions, so to speak, it can be inclusive and exclusive at the same moment; many more will enter the school than will ever complete a scenario, let alone sell one, and fewer still will have one produced by the school itself. The student can nonetheless feel a glow of pride as he or she passes through each wicket on the way to greater recognition, and even the unsuccessful can feel that they have gained something through their more fortunate fellow students.

At the time of the release of its first 'Palmerplay', *Judgment of the Storm*, the Corporation's students were urged to write to their local theatres to ask that the film be booked there, thereby contributing to the film's commercial success. Invoking the rhetoric of democracy that allows students to experience success vicariously, Manker asserted of *Judgment of the Storm* (in an open letter to other students) that 'It is your picture as much as the author's or ours, because it was written by one of your fellow students and produced by our institution',[51] suggesting that despite the emphasis on individual professional achievement, one of the course's main aims was to foster a sense of kinship among filmgoers by allowing them arenas for concerted action.

Recognition in this highly collaborative medium may have its price, however, because while greater and greater mastery of self-expression should lead to the further development of the self or 'personality', it may also have the effect of submerging it to some degree. Students succeed, presumably, because they have heeded the guidelines, mastered the jargon, and sent their manuscripts out flying the Palmer colours. But even should the story be produced, there may be some lingering doubt as to whose narrative it finally is.

Take, for instance, *Variety's* generally glowing review of the first effort in the Palmerplay production line:

> *Judgment of the Storm* if exploited properly should have no trouble cashing in. It is a Palmer Production produced by the Palmer Photoplay Corp., made up of former newspaper men, evidently with plenty of money and who threaten to be heard from if they keep up the same pace.
>
> The story is a first effort, written by Ethel Styles Middleton, described in the billing as a simple and domestic housewife of Pittsburgh. From the workmanlike construction of the story and the many old but always effective and clever tricks of the trade utilized, it seems likely that the 'housewife' business is merely bait, or possibly that some experienced, crafty rewrite man fixed the plot up to suit himself.[52]

Ironically, the very methods designed to bring success to the novice scenarist are those that apparently work to undermine his or her individuality. Another irony is that the three Palmer productions reviewed in *Variety* have a group flavour; it is their tendency toward melodrama of the kind that students are advised to avoid. *Judgment of the Storm* features *Way Down East*-like moments, relying on a big storm for some of its most stirring effects. The second film, *The White Sin*, is 'swift moving, dramatic and convincing except in one or two spots. The author found it necessary to work in a fire and rescue to plant his hero and heroine for the final embrace'.[53] By the time of the third Palmer release, *His Forgotten Wife*, the reviewer becomes positively impatient, declaring the film 'another of those amnesia and long arm of coincidence pictures, filled with the ancient hokum of the film business, to wit, two women after one man, automobile chases, the daring of the good woman to help the man she loves, the old family lawyer, and numerous clinch scenes'.[54]

The reliance on formula for success seemed to undermine not only the production of personality (whose is the successful picture, anyway?) but also the avowed purpose of the corporation's move into film manufacture. The object was to showcase fresh authorial talent and to reward the independent author through royalties.[55] Indeed, the best way of describing the Palmer foray into the making of actual movies is to liken it to a kind of 'Eminent Authors' program for unknowns. Poised on the knife edge of a number of warring approaches, then, the Palmer film production project exposes the awkwardly opposed aspects of the rhetoric surrounding the film industry. On the one hand, film is a democratic art and anyone can enter it. On the other, it requires both training and talent. It is a failing of the amateur to fall back on the creaky devices that were old when stage melodrama was young. Nonetheless, the experienced staff approving pictures for production appears to be selecting just those stories with the hoary aspects that so offend *Variety's* reviewer. Authorship is about lone creativity, some might say, although the film production process requires the collaboration of many, and the reviews of these pictures chiefly imply that the good, hard-working casts are the most important element in putting the weak stories over.

Finally, and perhaps most importantly, the Palmerplays intervene directly and quirkily in the debate raging over film's destiny as either adapter of material from other sources (novels, the stage,

magazines) or producer of original narratives. The value of the pre-sold property was a major topic of debate and analysis in the early 1920s, and reliance on it was often attributed either to the structure of film distribution or, in some instances, to the low caliber of audience taste. Because film was so expensive to produce, it had to exploit reliable and already extant markets. For example, Tamar Lane noted in 1923 that when [a producer] ... offers $5,000 or $125,000 for the rights to some noted play or book it is not because the story has any particular merit. It is purely because he feels that the particular story will draw big gate receipts. Many are the works the movie impresario buys at high rates of which he has never even read three lines. But he has heard it talked of in public and that is sufficient.[56]

This debate was not merely a feature of the trade papers; Palmer students were obliged to contemplate this aspect of film production through their reading of *Photodramatist*. Like Lane (who wrote for *Motion Picture Magazine* and *The Screen*), Rob Wagner deplored the expense of big adaptations and the recourse to stories culled from other media as a hedge against failure. Wagner carries on an imaginary conversation between the production managers in California and the distribution managers in New York, with the latter saying, 'The story is good and we feel that it will be a splendid vehicle for you, but can't you induce Wagner to shoot it into a magazine as our salesmen can get a much bigger price from exhibitors if the story has first appeared in a national magazine'.[57] On the other hand, Wagner bemoans film's reliance on unappealing or unseemly works from other media. He presents arguments on both sides of the original/adaptation divide, with the evidence more or less weighted toward the pre-sold property based on his understanding of the structure of film finance and distribution. Nonetheless, he concludes that originals will become the wave of the future because they must – film's high destiny as an art form requires that they do.[58]

This debate was not merely about suckering students into believing that there was room for them in an industry that had become by the early 1920s hierarchical and closed to the unconnected, untrained, and naive. The debate also manifested discomfort with certain structural aspects of the film

Fig. 5. Promotion for the novelisation of *Judgment of the Storm* [courtesy of Janet Staiger].

industry at the highest levels, which Will Hays spent a good deal of effort trying to assuage, often in rhetoric as strained as any appearing in Palmer publications. While the pre-sold property is a rational attempt to defray the costs of production and distribution by capitalising on the familiar, it involves the film industry directly in invidious comparisons with the publishing industry, which had constitutional protections that film lacked. As Richard Maltby observes, Hays's avowed desire to 'prevent the prevalent type of book and play from becoming the prevalent type of picture' was not the outward and visible sign of an inward and spiritual failure of taste, but rather a recognition that without constitutional protections, the film industry could only adapt works from other media in such a way as to minimise objectionable features; forgoing adaptation altogether was simply not an option.[59]

Despite its emphasis on the rhetoric of independence from the publishing establishment, then, Palmer likewise participated in a form of vassalage to the publishing industry through its strategy of 'novelising' *Judgment of the Storm*. Doubleday, Page & Company published the novel version at the time of the film's release in January 1924. This edition of the photoplay contained not only the novel proper but also the cutting script (hailed as a novelty) and stills from the film, permitting the publisher to call it the 'professional' edition. Needless to say, Palmer urged its purchase on the grounds that it would make an admirable textbook for the aspiring scenarist; again, the way to take bold new steps in changing one's career, and by extension one's self, is to imitate what others have done earlier.

But at the same time, the cutting script is described in such a way as to urge the taking up of screenwriting as a form of social mastery:

> This cutting script unquestionably represents the most important and fascinating phase of film production. It regulates the editing of the film. It exercises judgment over the story, direction, photography, research and every detail involved in the production of the picture. It packs dramatic action, recorded on miles of film, into a few thousand feet.[60]

In short, the script itself is presented as a kind of hero of the personality age – fascinating, efficient, authoritative, dynamic. Significantly, it can be possessed. It is a physical artefact from a culture most of whose manifestations are renowned for their ephemeral nature, another point the advertising takes pains to stress: 'The story is a faithful, permanent elaboration of the photoplay which, unfortunately, must flit across the silver screens of the country and be lost.'[61]

Moreover, this hybrid work of fiction again illuminates the vexing problem of authorship when the power and aims of a corporation are advising and directing the would be author. Middleton is not the 'author' of this work in its permanent physical form. Instead, the author of *Judgment of the Storm* the novel is Roy Mason, so that novelisation may work to undermine the new-found screen author in favour of the more experienced literary hack. In addition, the strategy of the novelisation is in line with the industry's desire to limit risk through the exploitation of pre-sold properties. The novelisation turns Middleton's idea into a kind of pre-sold property in which her name is not the most significant. Indeed, Palmer students are urged to read the book before they attend the film, thus making the film a pre-sold property after the fact.

Even pre-sold properties and the enthusiasm of the student body were evidently not enough to keep the production project afloat after the summer of 1924, and indeed it is perfectly possible that Palmer entered film production largely to shore up its market as correspondence school, as *Variety* and Sargent accused it of doing.[62] The Film Booking Office distributed the pictures, which seem not to have made a big impression on the industry, especially after the much-heralded first release, which was evidently the best of the lot. While the early and mid-1920s saw substantial economic consolidation in the film industry, particularly in exhibition and distribution, there were a number of small independent producers maneuvering within a market that still had room for them. Those conditions were gone by the end of the decade, but in the early 1920s Palmer might reasonably have thought that film production could bring benefits beyond increased enrolment or the gratification of those already enroled. In any event, Palmer could argue that it was already providing sales opportunities to its students by allowing them to place short story versions of their photoplay ideas in the house organ, which was known as the *Story World and Photodramatist* by the time the film production scheme was launched.

Because of Palmer's protean nature, it is difficult at times to identify in any limited way exactly what it was selling, a feature that its thoughtful choice of rhetoric only intensified. The firm may be said to be hawking variously a mystique, an adjunct

"Take them, John. Take all three of them! First kiss me! Then leave me! Take them and go!"

JUDGMENT OF
THE STORM

BY
ROY MASON

BASED ON THE PHOTOPLAY BY
ETHEL STYLES MIDDLETON
AS PRODUCED BY
PALMER PHOTOPLAY CORPORATION

GARDEN CITY   NEW YORK
DOUBLEDAY, PAGE & COMPANY
1923

Fig. 6. A scene from *Judgment of the Storm*: 'Take them, John. Take all three of them! Then leave me! take them and go!' used as the frontispiece of the novelisation.

education, a set of experiences, membership in an elect community, filmgoing *tout court*, specific films of its own manufacture, and even 'tools'. The importance of this last item is demonstrated by a startling description of the efficacy of the *Photoplay Plot Encyclopedia*, which student and produced author Martha Lord praises in terms that might be as appropriate to a drain cleaner:

> In plot construction the Palmer Photoplay Encyclopedia is invaluable – really, I have been able to work out the most unique situations through its aid. I keep it constantly by me and whenever I get my characters into such a predicament that an easy death seems the only solution of the problem, I delve into its pages, and presto! the plot uncoils.[63]

Given Palmer's definition of a photoplay story ('getting the characters into a predicament and then getting them out of it'),[64] the *Encyclopedia* was clearly an essential tool. In fostering the appeal of physical artefacts associated with film, the corporation, like the film industry at large, seems to promote a deliberate confusion between being and having, doing and appearing.

The case of writer and Palmer employee Frances White Elijah is similarly instructive because it suggests that some of what was at stake in learning about screenwriting was the easy appearance of connection to a glamorous career. Elijah describes the charm of representing oneself as a scenarist in this vignette in the *Photoplaywright*:

> One afternoon I was comfortably sitting on a country club porch, idly gazing into space and

wondering whether it was lack of energy or incentive that was causing me to waste a perfectly good afternoon instead of doing something worth while. As I sat there, an intelligent looking young chap of my acquaintance strolled along. He concluded his greeting with the prosaic question, 'What are you doing?' Any one could plainly see I was waiting for some one to offer me a cup of tea, but I felt the need of giving some kind of startling reply that would make an impression, so I answered: 'I am thinking up a new plot for a scenario'. It had the desired effect. He dropped into a nearby chair in astonishment.[65]

Clearly, the appeal of this profession is that it can transmute the lead of ill-spent leisure into the gold of success, or, at the very least, of public regard. In other words, the erstwhile film consumer can suddenly stand revealed as a producer, toiling on behalf of the industry even at a country club. If the correspondence schools overstated their ability to aid students in any material way, some students may have been satisfied with the possible rise in status that merely claiming connection with the enterprise would secure them. The desire to appear knowledgeable about technical aspects of the film world must have been widely dispersed in the 1920s, to judge from the extraordinary number of publications from this period that include glossaries of film terms for the lay person.

Mastering this new technological language might, by itself, have been enough for some subscribers. If technical vocabulary did not sate one's appetite for learning, the remarkable range of reference employed in the various Palmer lectures suggests that a desire to complete an inadequate education was another strong motive. For example, *The Point of Attack, or How to Start the Photoplay* invokes Gustave Flaubert and Alexandre Dumas *père* as exemplars or purveyors of advice. *Dramatic Suspense in the Photoplay* employs Gustav Freytag and Henrik Ibsen to make its points and develop its examples.[66] When we consider that these lectures are also liberally larded with references to photoplays such as *The Miracle Man* and Corbaley's *Gates of Brass*, we understand that part of what is at stake in the Palmer Plan is the ratification of filmgoing and of the filmgoer's taste. Film, when it

lives up to the high destiny predicted for it, will produce works that can be mentioned in the same breath as those penned by the most august (and daring) nineteenth-century masters of the novel and the drama.

Education was not the major indicator of success in a decade that typically measured achievement in terms of how much money that achievement might realise; as Frederick Palmer himself pointed out, the job is 'to write and SELL stories'.[67] But the Plan still had something to offer the individual and the industry even if not every student could hope to attain the status of professional author. Given the frequent recourse to notions of audience inadequacy as an explanation for film's failure to rise to the artistic heights predicted for it, some program of 'audience education' would have appeared to be well advised. Writing for Palmer students, Douglas Z. Doty noted:

> It is significant that so many people are engaged in attempting to write for the screen; and already there has been a curious reaction. Few of these writers are commercially successful, but it is distinctly noticeable that the average motion picture audience is growing much more critical of what it sees, and this is bound to have a salutary effect on the productions of the future.[68]

More precisely, *Photodramatist* advised Palmer students that 'although the student should fail to sell a single story, the broad mental training received in studying the course should prove of advantage in meeting the world at any angle'.[69]

Much of the Palmer advertising emphasised the latent potential for success rather than the reality – sound business practice when the latter cannot be guaranteed. Some of the advertising, to be sure, indulged in the *Bildungsroman* of the unhappy housewife, clerk, or minister who rises to power and fame through screenwriting. When a Palmer advertisement asked potential students, 'Have *you* the power that makes some men and women great?', it clearly hoped to harness the general enthusiasm for mastery that crops up in so many 1920s advertisements to the specific desire to achieve fame through screenwriting.[70] 'Creative imagination' is the tool that will best assist students, and it is strangely general in its application: 'It is the force that solves most of life's problems; that builds great dams, factories, and universities; that produces x-rays and radio; that writes masterpieces of literature.' It is no accident that every example but one belongs to the world of industry, science, or corporate life. In promoting a Taylorised formula for the production of screenplays – indeed, a kind of Taylorisation of self-expression – the Palmer Photoplay Corporation may have worked to reconcile students to their fates as members of large industrial enterprises. A better 'educated' audience, one with some mastery of the technology of film production, could be represented as in some way leading to better films through its more critical appreciation.

At the same time, however, it was an audience given an excuse to consume more films, simply because it hoped to have a hand in producing them. The most consistently repeated piece of advice to the would-be scenarist, not only among the Palmer materials but also among trade papers and fan magazines, was to see as many movies as possible, as many times as possible. This advice acknowledges that the demonstration of technique in order to encourage amateur production could also discourage such participation in Hollywood even as it appeared to provoke it, thus relegating the audience to the position of better-informed consumer. More specifically, books and articles designed to show what an arduous and dignified craft screenwriting really is elevated the social cachet of filmmaking and filmgoing, but they also channelled and controlled discontent over the quality of films and the nature of the film industry. Students were advised not to say that they could make better movies until they had tried to do so themselves.

Finally, as the form of Taylorised artistic production par excellence, Hollywood is famous for the dispersal or occlusion of authorship within picture manufacture. Perhaps the most important issue that the Palmer Photoplay Corporation throws into relief is that this dispersion of authorship not only involved a wide variety of crafts within the industry (each of which could claim some 'authority' through its collaboration with the more conventional notion of author), but involved the distribution of the function of author to film audiences as well. ♠

Acknowledgement

I would like to thank Janet Staiger for graciously making available to me her collection of Palmer Photoplay Corporation materials, and John Belton for his helpful suggestions for the revision of this article.

Notes

1. Sinclair Lewis, *Babbitt* (New York: Signet, 1980), 65.

2. Examples of these schools include the Photoplay Enterprise Association in Boonville, Indiana (evidently consisting of a single book sent through the mail for $1.50, authored by Monte Katterjohn); the Home Correspondence School in Springfield, Massachusetts, which published *Writer's Monthly*, among other titles; and the Manhattan Motion Picture Institute in New York, which was the sponsor of Florence Radinoff's *The Photoplaywright's Handy Text-Book* (1913).

3. By 1925, an MPPDA publication on screenwriting ('Facts About Scenario Writing', *Motion Picture* 1.3, November 1925: 2–4) noted that a number of studios had announced that they no longer accepted unsolicited submissions owing to the risk of litigation that such manuscripts presented; studios wished neither to be duped into producing plagiarised work nor to be accused of having stolen the work of unknown authors. For the elaborate precautions studios were taking by the late 1920s to avoid such suits, see 'Unsolicited Manuscripts Not Read', *Variety* (22 August 1928): 6; for an account of a costly suit, see '$500,000 Sought by Woman in Alleged Film Piracy', *Variety* (1 June 1926): 4. Part of the concern with plagiarism during this period was a holdover from the early 1910s, when it was possible to submit an idea to a studio without going to the labour of writing a scenario or even a full-scale treatment; as late as 1918, Thomas Ince spoke in 'The Undergraduate and the Scenario' (*Bookman*, June 1918: 416) of buying 'first-class stories that have been written on the back of a single envelope'. But in reality, such informal submissions were exceedingly rare by the 1920s because studios had developed scenario departments and captured a great deal of authorial labour through contracts. They were no longer willing to pay merely for good ideas and gimmicks designed to refresh hackneyed plots.

4. Frederick Palmer, *Photoplay Plot Encyclopedia* (Hollywood: Palmer Photoplay Corporation, 1922), 3. The Palmer house organ was variously called *The Photoplaywright* (1919–21), *The Photodramatist* and *Photodramatist* (1921–23), and *The Story World and Photodramatist* (1923 on). Starting in

June 1921, the journal was the 'official organ of the Screen Writers' Guild of the Authors' League of America' (Ted LeBerthon, 'This Side of Nirvana', *The Photodramatist*, June 1921): 13.

5. The first instalment was evidently $15 (Palmer Photoplay Corporation, *Little Stories of Success*, Los Angeles, 1922, 4). See also Palmer subscription brochures, n.d., in the collection of Richard Koszarski.

6. *Photoplay* (February 1919): 96.

7. '$500 for His First Photoplay – Thanks to the Palmer Plan', *Photoplay* (April 1919): 98, and 'Your Movie Ideas Are Worth Big Money IF –', *Photoplay* (May 1919): 98.

8. 'New Novelist Discovered in a Department Store', *Writer's Monthly* (March 1925): 275.

9. Janet Staiger, '"Tame" Authors and the Corporate Laboratory: Stories, Writers, and Scenarios in Hollywood', *Quarterly Review of Film Studies* 8.4 (Fall 1983): 34–35. Staiger focuses particularly on the incorporation of authorship into the studio system, either through the establishment of scenario departments (starting by 1912 or even earlier) or through the securing of an author's services by contract.

10. The Emerson/Loos series appeared from February to July 1918 in *Photoplay*, and was subsequently published as *How to Write Photoplays* (1920). Frederic Arnold Kummer's 'The Rejected One' may be found in *Photoplay* (March 1918): 45–49ff.

11. Edward Azlant, *The Theory, History, and Practice of Screenwriting, 1897–1920,* (unpublished Ph.D. dissertation, University of Wisconsin, Madison, 1980), 104.

12. William Lord Wright, 'Photoplay Authors Real and Near', *New York Dramatic Mirror* (9 September 1916): 43.

13. 'Florida Woman Wins Scenario Contest Conducted by Goldwyn and Newspaper', *Moving Picture World* (15 April 1922): 721.

14. 'An Open Letter to Those Who Desire to Write Scenarios, But Have Never Received the Palmer Questionnaire', *Photodramatist* (July 1922): 4. Given that Palmer claims to have sold some $60,000 worth of scenarios by this time, it is possible that contest prizes constituted a fairly high proportion of the money earned by students (Fritz Tidden, 'Keeping in Personal Touch', *Moving Picture World*, 10 June 1922: 553.)

15. Sheldon Krag Johnson, 'Breaking in from the Top: A Review of the $10,000 Prize Photoplay "Broken Chains"', *Photodramatist* (January 1923): 21.

16. Frederick Palmer, *Author's Fiction Manual* (Hollywood: Palmer Institute of Authorship, 1924), ix.

17. Walter Benn Michaels, 'An American Tragedy, or the Promise of American Life', *Representations* 25 (Winter 1989): 73.

18. *Little Stories of Success*, 16.

19. Hamilton Wayne, 'Breaking the Shackles of Silence', *Overland Monthly and Out West Magazine* (July 1925): 258–259.

20. Warren Susman, *Culture as History: The Transformation of American Society in the Twentieth Century* (New York: Pantheon, 1984), 277.

21. Frederick Palmer, *The Essentials of Photoplay Writing* (Los Angeles: Palmer Photoplay Corporation, 1921), 5; emphasis in the original.

22. Frederick Palmer, *Palmer Plan Handbook* (Los Angeles: Palmer Photoplay Corporation, 1921), 10.

23. David Bordwell, for example, cites Frederick Palmer's distinction between movement and action (appearing in his *Technique of the Photoplay*, 1924) as a useful instance of the theory behind story causality within the classical Hollywood cinema (David Bordwell, Janet Staiger, and Kristin Thompson, *The Classical Hollywood Cinema: Film Style and Mode of Production to 1960,* New York: Columbia University Press, 1985, 15).

24. On the importance of action, see, for example, 'What Is a Photoplay?' (Frederick Palmer, *Palmer Plan Handbook*, Los Angeles: Palmer Photoplay Corporation, 1918, 12–15). Examples of other lectures involving aspects of technique include George Beban, *Photoplay Characterization* (Los Angeles: Palmer Photoplay Corporation, 1920), and Denison Clift, *Dramatic Suspense in the Photoplay* (Los Angeles: Palmer Photoplay Corporation, 1920).

25. *Palmer* (1918), 51.

26. Elizabeth Peltret, 'My Experience in an Academy of Motion Picture Art', *Photoplay* (February 1919): 57–58. For the MPPDA crackdown on fraudulent schemes, see 'Hays After Film Fakers', *Variety* (20 December 1923): 1.

27. Epes Winthrop Sargent, 'Flimflamming the Film Fans', *Woman's Home Companion* (November 1924): 26ff.

28. Sargent, 26.

29. See, for example, Alfred Hustwick's proposals in 'Motion Pictures – To-day and To-morrow: 5 – A Plan to Revive the Motion Picture Art', *The Film*

Spectator (11 December 1926): 13. Hustwick calls for more systematic study of motion picture manufacture, including the establishment of a research bureau in each studio and closer relations with universities and colleges.

30. *Little Stories of Success*, 16.

31. *Little Stories of Success*, 16.

32. I include Francis White Elijah, who was employed by Palmer as manager of its New York office ('Palmer Photoplay Opens Office in New York City', *Moving Picture World*, 11 February 1922: 613). Elijah was profiled in *The Photoplaywright* as a particularly interesting success story (Elijah, 'How It Happened', April 1921): 3.

33. Manker complained that although women made up only 40 per cent of the enrolment of the school, their scenarios sold more readily (Mary Kelly, 'Do Dramas Cater Exclusively to Women? Roy L. Manker Sees Possible Danger', *Moving Picture World* 11 February 1922: 615). Much of the Palmer literature suggests that women were as valued a constituency as were men, however, and it is significant that their stories of success outnumber the men's. I have dealt with the issue of the gendering of screenwriting at greater length in '"Would You Be Ashamed to Let Them See What You Have Written?" The Gendering of Photoplaywrights, 1913–23', forthcoming in 1998 from *Tulsa Studies in Women's Literature*.

34. Frances Denton, 'Real Folks', *Photoplay* (April 1918): 83.

35. Kate Corbaley, *Selling Manuscripts in the Photoplay Market* (Los Angeles: Palmer Photoplay Corporation, 1920), 5–6.

36. Corbaley, 9.

37. Corbaley, 7–8. See also *The Essentials of Photoplay Writing*, which justifies the process by saying, 'This is done so all manuscripts will be uniform in appearance and instantly identified as Palmer Plan material. The quality of Palmer stories being thoroughly established, it is obvious that any synopsis submitted through us will receive immediate consideration' (19).

38. The concept of a Palmer brand is suggested by the text of the earliest advertisement that I have been able to locate: 'Scenarios that carry this stamp ['read and approved – Frederick Palmer'] are instantly recognized by producers, directors and editors as stories of unquestioned merit' (*New York Dramatic Mirror*, 21 September 1918: 457). The advertisement solicits both authors and producers.

39. *The Essentials of Photoplay Writing*, 31.

40. Corbaley, 9.

41. Palmer, *The Essentials of Photoplay Writing*, 11.

42. Letter appearing in the department 'Between Ourselves', the *Photodramatist* (April 1921): 13.

43. Ted LeBerthon, 'This Side of Nirvana', *The Photodramatist* (July 1921): 13.

44. For an example of these instructions, see Jeanie MacPherson, *The Necessity and Value of Theme in the Photoplay* (Los Angeles: Palmer Photoplay Corporation, 1920), 8–9.

45. It is impossible to determine how many students the school took out of all those that applied. It seems highly unlikely that any significant culling of applications took place. For example, Manker was quoted as 'predict[ing] the number of enrollments will be increased three to four thousand before the year [1920] is out' ('Palmerland', *Photoplaywright*, November 1920: 12). In June 1921, LeBerthon reported the circulation of *The Photodramatist* as 13,000 (12). It was possible to subscribe to the journal for $2.50 without joining the school.

46. Advertisement, *Photoplaywright* (January 1921): back cover.

47. Jeanne Stevens, 'Mediocre Pictures – the Remedy', *Photodramatist* (September 1922): 18.

48. Tidden, 553.

49. Palmer, *The Essentials of Photoplay Writing*, 5.

50. Palmer, *The Essentials of Photoplay Writing*, 4.

51. Roy L. Manker, undated circular letter to subscribers.

52. 'Judgment of the Storm' (31 January 1924), *Variety Film Reviews*, vol. 2 (New York: Garland, 1983).

53. 'The White Sin' (14 May 1924), *Variety Film Reviews*, vol. 2 (New York: Garland, 1983).

54. 'His Forgotten Wife' (25 June 1924), *Variety Film Reviews*, vol. 2 (New York: Garland, 1983).

55. The terms for *Judgment of the Storm*, for example, were a minimum 'advance royalty' of $1000 and some unspecified further fraction of the profits ('Palmer Photoplay Corporation Enters Film Producing Field', circular sent to students during the summer of 1922, n.d.).

56. Tamar Lane, *What's Wrong with the Movies?* (Los Angeles: The Waverley Co., 1923), 42.

57. Rob Wagner, 'Nailing a Fallacy', *The Photoplaywright* (January 1921): 3.

58. Wagner, 3.

59. Richard Maltby, 'To Prevent the Prevalent Type of Book', *Movie Censorship and American Culture*, ed. Francis G. Couvares (Washington: Smithsonian Institution Press, 1996), 100–103.

60. 'Send No Money to Get This Book', undated Palmer Photoplay circular, n.p.

61. 'Send No Money to Get This Book', n.p.

62. See 'His Forgotten Wife', *Variety Film Reviews*, which dismisses the last picture as 'one of the series of yarns produced by the Palmer Photoplay School as an inducement to show those who take their scenario courses that there is a production chance for the work they turn out after paying to learn how it is done'. Sargent argues that the production scheme more than pays for itself: 'The company using this idea loses no money; in fact it is reputed to have cleaned up more than a million dollars in the past few years' ('Flimflamming the Film Fans', 26). Given that Palmerplays had been in production for only a year at this point, however, most of those profits must have come from instruction fees.

63. '"The Inner Sight" Is Sold to Ince for $500', *The Photoplaywright* (October 1920): 7.

64. *Palmer Plan Handbook* (1918), 58.

65. Elijah, 3.

66. Clarence G. Badger, *The Point of Attack, or How to Start the Photoplay* (Los Angeles: Palmer Photoplay Corporation, 1920); Clift, *Dramatic Suspense in the Photoplay*.

67. *Palmer Plan Handbook* (1918), 18.

68. Douglas Z. Doty, 'The Unpublished Author: A Plea for the Cultural Value of Learning to Write', *Photodramatist* (November 1922): 20.

69. Theodore Moracin, 'The Transmuters of Dreams', *The Photodramatist* (June 1921): 15.

70. 'Have You the Power That Makes Some Men and Women Great?' *Photodramatist* (October 1922): 36.

Film History, Volume 9, pp. 320–332, 1997. Copyright © John Libbey & Company
ISSN: 0892-2160. Printed in Australia

Charles Bennett and the typical Hitchcock scenario

John Belton

The credits of Alfred Hitchcock's first talking picture read 'Blackmail ... From the play by Charles Bennett'. Hitchcock and Bennett subsequently collaborated on a string of extremely successful pictures for Gaumont British, including *The Man Who Knew Too Much* (1934), *The 39 Steps* (1935), *The Secret Agent* (1936), *Sabotage* (1936) and *Young and Innocent* (1937). One of Hitchcock's first efforts in Hollywood, *Foreign Correspondent* (1940), was also written by Bennett; and, of course, Hitchcock's remake of *The Man Who Knew Too Much* (1956) credits Bennett with the original story. Hitchcock's work with Bennett occurred at a crucial time in the director's career, when he began to achieve international recognition and when his films regularly began to secure distribution in the United States.

Hitchcock's other English films are, of course, necessarily 'Hitchcockian', but it is during this period of collaboration with Bennett that one form or type of what has been identified as the 'typical Hitchcock scenario' emerges.[1] It is the story of the innocent character (or characters, as in *The Man Who Knew Too Much*) suddenly plunged into an espionage plot or suspected of murder. As Charles Bennett put it in describing *The 39 Steps*, it is the story of 'the guy on the run with the heavies out to get him because he knows the truth and the police are also out to get him before the heavies do because the police think he's the murderer'.[2] Bennett helped craft this story formula.

The second of three sons, Bennett was born at Shoreham-on-Sea in Sussex on 2 August 1899. He died on 15 June 1995, at the age of 95. The author of more than 50 produced screenplays, he received

the Screen Laurel Award from the Writers Guild of America in 1995. During his long career, he worked repeatedly with directors Robert Stevenson, Cecil B. DeMille, John Sturges, Jacques Tourneur and Irwin Allen. At the age of 91, he was still writing: he had been hired by Twentieth Century-Fox producers Stuart Birnbaum and William Blaylock, to write a script for a remake of *Blackmail*.[3] The Screen Laurel Award notes that 'he has made a distinctive and indelible impression on the art of the cinema both here and abroad, and his work will endure as a testament to the craft of writing'.[4]

Bennett's father died when he was four. His mother, Lillian Langrishe Bennett, subsequently became an actress and also produced a series of unsuccessful plays. Bennett began his career as a child actor, making his stage debut at the Olympia theatre on 23 December 1911, co-starring with Gertrude Lawrence in Max Reinhardt's production of Charles B. Cochran's *The Miracle*. In 1915, he played young John Halifax in George Pearson's film *John Halifax, Gentleman* (his only screen appearance except for an uncredited walk-on in *The 39 Steps*).[5] In 1917–18, he served in France. After the war, he toured with the Compton Comedy company (1920) and the Lena Ashwell Players (1922) and appeared in several productions staged in London's

John Belton teaches film in the English Department at Rutgers, where he also occasionally offers a course in screenwriting. Correspondence should be sent to John Belton, 243 Baltic Street, Brooklyn, NY, 11201, USA

Fig. 1. Charles Bennett, 'distinguished screen playwright', in a 1949 whisky advertisement. [All illustrations from author's collection.]

West End. He began writing plays in 1925, while touring with the English Players in Paris. He retired from the stage as an actor in 1927 to become a full-time playwright.

Bennett's plays include *The Return* (1927, Everyman Theatre, London), *Blackmail* (1928, Globe Theatre, London), *The Last Hour* (1928, Comedy Theatre, London), *After Midnight* (1929, Rudolph Steiner, London), *The Danger Line* (co-authored with Hazel Marshall, 1930, Greenwich, CT), *Sensation* (1931, Lyceum Theatre, London), *Big Business* (1932, Beaux-Arts, Monte Carlo) and *Page From a Diary/Masquerade* (1936, Garrick Theatre, London).[6] *Blackmail* starred Tallulah Bankhead; *Page From a Diary* Greer Garson.

Bennett's plays can be seen, in part, as a product of Britain in the 1920s, as a mixture of pre-war idealism and post-war disillusionment. His charac-

ters are frequently caught in an awkward transition of values, like the heroine of *Blackmail*, whose Victorian sexual morality becomes a subject for debate for the Bohemian artist who, espousing the principles of free love, tries to seduce her. Similarly, the virtue of the innocent young couple in *The Danger Line* is assaulted by the more permissive Jazz Age sexual codes of two of their fellow weekenders at Lady (Charmian) Grantham's country estate.

A metaphysical drama dealing with the supernatural, *The Return* tells the story of a sheltered, wealthy young draftee, Eric Norcott, who is killed by a shell explosion in the trenches in France. Concerned for the health and happiness of his widowed mother, Eric's spirit refuses to leave his body until someone agrees to go and comfort his mother. The stillborn Ishtar (played on the stage by Bennett) is a spirit who has never lived. He takes Eric's place and returns to the little village in which his mother lives in order to spare her the grief of losing her only son.[7]

Bennett's semi-autobiographical play (one of his brothers died in the war) was dedicated 'to one of the glorious million – my brother – Gunner Eric Bennett, RFA, and to my mother whose name should rightly be on the title page'.[8] The well-meaning, idealistic and innocent Ishtar finds himself thrust into the midst of a series of scandals. Unaware that Eric has got a neighbouring farm girl (played by Peggy Ashcroft) pregnant, Ishtar refuses to marry her. Nor can he explain his sudden discharge from the army. Since he cannot explain his mysterious return home, Eric must be a deserter. Confronted by evidence of Eric's death, Ishtar remains unable to explain his presence as Eric. Like the Hitchcock hero wrongly blamed for the crimes of another, Ishtar finds that he is unable to defend himself. He can only appeal to the faith of others in him, imploring the mother to believe him without proof. As a result, both he and she become ostracised by the rest of the village. Ishtar ultimately redeems himself by confessing that he is an imposter and by reconciling Eric's mother with the girl who will bear Eric's child. The overtly spiritualistic play is all about faith, about belief without knowledge, a theme that Bennett shares with Hitchcock.

More generally, the play deals with the difficulties of post-war readjustment to civilian life faced by the veteran, whether he be whole, crippled, or shell-shocked. The man who returns, i.e. Ishtar, is not the same man (Eric) who went to war, though he resembles him in appearance. In its concern for doubles, substitutions, and the wrongly accused innocent, *The Return* directly foreshadows Bennett's later work with Hitchcock (the wrongly accused Hannay in *The 39 Steps*, Caypor in *Secret Agent*, and Tisdale in *Young and Innocent*, as well as Van Meer's double substitute in *Foreign Correspondent*). Yet the story is Bennett's. It is dedicated to his mother and to his brother Eric, who was killed in France during the war and whose name becomes that of the dead hero. The self-destructive refusal of Ishtar, and of subsequent Bennett heroes and heroines, to explain himself may also have an autobiographical counterpart in the person of Vere, Bennett's younger brother. At the height of his career as a theatrical producer, Vere committed suicide (in 1926, a year before the play opened).

Whether its source is artistic or autobiographical, *The Return* is dominated by a sense of loss; it is this theme which characterises Bennett's best work in the theatre and on the screen.

Hitchcock once observed that 'Charles Bennett … is essentially a writer of melodrama'.[9] By 'melodrama', Hitchcock presumably means dramas centred around moral conflict. *The Return* clearly focussed itself on the hero's moral dilemma – a desire to comfort the mother of the dead soldier whose place he takes versus the potential scandal of his return, which raises issues of dereliction of duty (his responsibility to Mary, whom Eric had got pregnant, and his apparent desertion from the army). The moral dilemma is, quite roughly, that between love and duty. As Hitchcock himself has often pointed out, this dilemma lies at the heart of *Blackmail*, in which the detective hero is torn between his responsibility as a police officer and his love for his girlfriend, who has committed a murder.[10]

Bennett's play is built around this dilemma; however, Bennett's version of *Blackmail* differs significantly from Hitchcock's 1929 film version. His heroine, Alice Jarvis (not White), a department store salesgirl, is torn between her Victorian upbringing and her attraction to the Bohemian world of post-war London. When she tells the artist, Peter Hewitt, that she wants to remain a virgin for her future husband, he tells her she is old-fashioned and that 'we chucked over the conventions of Queen Victoria years ago'.[11] They struggle; she stabs him in the back and in the throat with a bread knife; he falls to the floor dead.

When she returns home later the next day, she refuses to tell her parents where she was. They suspect her of having slept with a man. She merely says, 'Whatever *did* happen is a thousand times worse than anything you can imagine'. Her silence resembles Ishtar's: unable to confide in others, she is forced into an inner world of torment and anguish.

Alice's boyfriend, Harold Webber, investigates the murder for Scotland Yard, finds her gloves at the scene of the crime, and forces her to confess to him. After her confession, Harold comforts her, telling her 'I'll stick by you, Alice … We're the only two in the world who will *ever* know'.[12] At that moment, the doorbell rings and the blackmailer, Ian Tracy, enters.

Fig. 2. Anny Ondra as Alice White in Hitchcock's version of *Blackmail* (BIP, 1929).

Tracy is later suspected of the murder. Harold, who is quite a bit more ruthless in the play than in the film, is delighted. He says to Alice, 'Let 'em [hang Tracy] ... What does it matter ... swine like that? And the evidence will be against him, too. It doesn't matter *what* he says. It'll only be *his* word against yours.'[13] Alice, however, prays for Tracy to escape. She feeds and shelters him when he runs from the police; she identifies with him when he tells how hunted he feels. Alice begs Harold to turn her in, threatening to confess if he doesn't. But Harold has another plan, saying he will kill Tracy and insist that the latter resisted arrest. Harold pulls his revolver, telling Tracy, 'Look at it, you swine. Murder to cover murder. It's been done before, you know'.[14] In an attempt to prevent the shooting, Alice struggles with Harold for the gun. It goes off, but no one is hit. Alice's dilemma is finally resolved when Harold calls the station house and learns that police doctors have discovered that the artist had a heart condition and died of a heart attack. 'What a lot of fools we've been', declares Harold. 'Why the wound wasn't deep enough to have killed. The jugular vein wasn't touched. He died ... of HEART FAILURE!'[15]

The endings of Bennett's plays tend to involve *deus ex machina* solutions, rescuing essentially innocent characters from the consequences of their momentary lapses into sin or crime. Thus miraculous reversals conclude *Blackmail* and *The Last Hour*. his characters are rescued not through the success of their own efforts but through irrational, divine intervention. This logic governs the resolutions of a number of scripts Bennett wrote for Hitchcock. In *Secret Agent*, the British spies repeatedly bungle efforts to complete their assignment and kill the German spy. The German spy dies at the end by accident in a train wreck.[16] The hero thus retains his innocence, though he remains indirectly responsible for the death of an innocent man. At the end of *Sabotage*, a bomb explodes in a movie theatre and miraculously destroys evidence of a murder committed by the film's heroine. She is thus technically 'absolved' of her guilt. The search for the real killer by the hero and heroine in *Young and Innocent* ends in failure, but an omniscient crane shot finds him and he betrays himself to the police, clearing the hero of all suspicion. Products of a post-war sensibility, Bennett and Hitchcock share an absurdist vision in which a powerless hero and or heroine is rescued by a melodramatic reversal of fortune.

Tallulah Bankhead insisted that Bennett's ending be rewritten for her when she played Alice on stage. Thus the version that Hitchcock probably saw at the Globe had no last-minute reprieve but ended with Alice giving herself up to the police.[17] Hitchcock's film has Tracy fall to his death from the roof of the British Museum while being pursued by police. The police assume Tracy killed the artist and, when Alice tries to confess to the crime, her boy-

friend stops her. The film leaves the guilty couple with the deaths of two men – the artist and the blackmailer – on their consciences. In Bennett's play morality is relative; guilt is the product of perception. Alice feels she is guilty only when she believes she committed a crime. Her guilt vanishes when she learns that she did not kill the artist. Hitchcock refuses to absolve her of her guilt. Morality is absolute; it is not a by-product of (false) perception.

After the release of *Blackmail*, Bennett adapted another of his plays, *The Last Hour*, which Walter Forde made into a film in 1930. Bennett's play is a spy thriller, set in the bar of an inn known as the 'Goat and Compasses' near Dartmoor prison. In a plot that foreshadows that of *The 39 Steps*, one of the characters (a German prince named Nichola) has stolen the plans for 'the most deadly invention the world has ever known ... Whitehall's most closely-guarded secret ... the Haviland Death Ray'.[18] (Bennett reports that the stage effects were quite spectacular: 'I actually had characters burned alive, instantaneously, in front of the audience's eyes by the death ray.')[19]

The play is built around a series of plot reversals, similar to those in *Secret Agent* in which the suspected spy is not a spy and a charming, apparently harmless character is. The plot resembles, in part, that of *The Man Who Knew Too Much*: a subplot explains that the spies have blackmailed the innkeeper, Tregellis, into helping them by concealing the whereabouts of his fugitive son, whom they have hidden away. The innkeeper's daughter, Mary, is played by Margaret Riddick, who subsequently married Bennett. Like the police chief's daughter in *Young and Innocent*, Mary falls in love with a man who appears to be an escaped convict. The tightly plotted play ends with the death of the prince, who invokes diplomatic immunity and is about to escape when he is shot by Tregellis with the Death Ray. Tregellis, who is shot and appears to have been killed earlier in the play, returns from the dead to set things right at the end. The false death or return from the dead emerges as a central Bennett motif, found in *The Return, Blackmail, The Danger Line* and other Bennett story ideas. This motif serves as a major plot point in both *The 39 Steps*, in which Hannay feigns death to escape from Professor Jordan; in *Secret Agent*, which begins with the faking of Ashenden's (Gielgud's) death; and in

Foreign Correspondent, in which the diplomat Van Meer's death is faked in order to conceal his abduction.

The Danger Line (1930), co-authored with Hazel Marshall, also relies on a false death. Sylvia is ignored by her husband, Bobby, who finds Dolly Griffin more attractive. In retaliation, Sylvia invites the romantic Count Vesci to her room. When he tries to seduce her, she pushes him away. He falls and appears dead, like the artist in *Blackmail*, who is also 'killed' by the heroine in self-defence. Disenchanted by the blatant advances of Dolly, whom Bennett describes as 'a Messalina of eternally unsatisfied desires', Bobby discovers the Count's body. He carries it from her room back to the Count's, helping her cover up the crime much in the same way as the detective heroes of *Blackmail* and *Sabotage* do.

Sylvia pleads for Bobby to believe in her innocence (a Bennett motif that is also recurrent in Hitchcock), but he refuses. Bobby and Sylvia are a typical Hitchcock couple (see *Blackmail* and *Sabotage*), wedded to one another through a shared guilt. As Bobby says, 'there's a dead man between us for the rest of our lives'. The Count, who has a history of cataleptic attacks, descends from his room the next morning to set everything right, testifying to Sylvia's fidelity to her husband.

As with other Bennett plays, *The Danger Line* reflects a post-war, moral cynicism which challenges traditional values. Charmian, the hostess who oversees the weekend, articulates these in an attempt to rationalise her own behavior: 'We, of this generation, more than *any* others, have been face to face with the realities of life. We've known the horror of sudden death ... The devastating bolt from the blue. The world in our time is just a gigantic landslide and the best philosophy is to hold onto happiness with both hands if we're fortunate enough for it to come our way.'[20] This apocalyptic vision dominates Bennett's theatrical work and resurfaces repeatedly in Hitchcock's films of the 1930s in which an Old World order is overturned by a 'devastating bolt from the blue'. This scenario premise is often attributed to novelist John Buchan, who, back in 1913, wrote a story about a man named Lethen, who suddenly 'found himself pursued "like thief":' for no apparent reason down a London street. Lethan observed: 'I suddenly realised

how thin was the protection of civilisation!'[21] But it is a plot device that runs throughout Bennett's work as well.

Bennett did not work with Hitchcock on *Blackmail*, though he did meet the director during the shooting of the film. The success of the film prompted British International Pictures (BIP) to hire Bennett to write six stories a year for them. He was to present the stories in the form of six page treatments. After submitting a series of story ideas, Bennett asked for a screenwriting assignment and co-authored the script for *Hawleys of High Street* (1933) and other films before being assigned to work with Hitchcock.

BIP owned the rights to the Bulldog Drummond stories and the Bulldog Drummond character. They asked Bennett and Hitchcock to write an original story for the Bulldog Drummond character. Bennett came up with 'Bulldog Drumond's Baby', a story about Bulldog Drummond in Switzerland. Drummond stumbles onto a spy plot and the spies kidnap his baby to keep him quiet. BIP did not make the picture. When Hitchcock moved to Gaumont British, he took the story with him. Since BIP owned the Drummond character, Hitchcock and Bennett changed Drummond into the semi-anonymous figure of Bob Lawrence, a typical, middle-class Englishman who gets ensnared in a complex spy plot while vacationing with his wife and daughter in St Moritz. The story, in which a villain blackmails the hero and heroine into silence, reworks the plot of *Blackmail*. The dilemma emerges as the familiar conflict between love and duty. The Lawrences are forced to choose between the welfare of their child and that of a foreign dignitary, between paternal feelings and their sense of duty to the state.

In this film, the love versus duty conflict is satisfactorily resolved. The couple save the dignitary and rescue their child. The mother, Jill Lawrence, actually saves her daughter by shooting one of her kidnappers on a roof at the end.

Bennett's strengths as a screenwriter lay more in his ability to construct story action, to write treatments and continuities, than in his talent for writing dialogue. *The 39 Steps* is a case in point. The project began with Bennett preparing a short treatment of Buchan's novella.[22] Retaining only Buchan's central story idea of the innocent man pursued by both the police and a ring of spies, Bennett and Hitchcock invented a series of places and people around

SMOOTH... SUAVE... SOFT SPOKEN... CHARMING... GRACIOUS... COURTLY
... and the most cold blooded murderer in all the history of crime.

NOVA PILBEAM
PETER LORRE
LESLIE BANKS
EDNA BEST

THE MAN WHO KNEW TOO MUCH

DIRECTED BY ALFRED HITCHCOCK

A GB PRODUCTION

Fig. 3. A lobby card for *The Man Who Knew Too Much* (GB, 1934).

which to organise hero Hannay's adventures. They also built the story around the developing romance between the hero and a woman who initially refuses to believe in his innocence. Buchan's story has no love interest.

Buchan's plot involved an assassination attempt (as in *The Man Who Knew Too Much*) and a threatened invasion of England. Drawing on *The Last Hour*, this was changed to the theft of plans for a secret weapon from the War Ministry with the intention of smuggling these plans out of the country. In need of a character to 'copy' the plans and of a device to use to get them out of the country, Bennett came up with 'Mr Memory', a character similar to the phoney mindreader he had just worked on with director Maurice Elvey for *The Clairvoyant* (1934). (Buchan's spy *may* have memorised the plans for the defence of England; no one can tell for sure.)

The catalyst for Buchan's story, a dead spy

named Franklin Scudder, who lives in Hannay's building, becomes the mysterious Anabella Smith, whom he meets (along with Mr Memory) at the Music Hall. Here and in other instances, Bennett's plotting is tighter and more clearly driven by a cause-and-effect logic than Buchan's. Buchan's Hannay flees to Scotland in order to hide from the spies and the police. In the film, Bennett and Hitchcock plant a map of Scotland (with a circled location) on the body of the dead spy, deftly providing Hannay with motivation to go to Scotland and with a person to find there, the Professor, who might be able to help him prove his innocence. Once in Scotland, Hannay discovers that the Professor is an enemy spy and follows him back to London. In Buchan, Hannay finally convinces government officials of the spy plot and they help him track down and capture the chief spy, who is hiding somewhere on the English coast, at a house with 39 steps leading down to a small cove from which he plans to escape.

Bennett and Hitchcock's final construction of a narrative sequence is classically ordered according to principles of symmetry. It moves from England to Scotland and back to England again; from City to Country to City. The first scene takes place in a theatre (the Music Hall), as does the last (the Palladium). Mr Memory (and his music) appears in both, and in both a shot is fired. In the centre of the film, a shot is fired again – this time at Hannay, who appears to die but who has been saved by the hymnal in his coat pocket. A classical odyssey, the hero 'dies', i.e. journeys to the underworld, and then returns home.

39 Steps

I. England (night one)
  1. City

    A. Music Hall
     London. Lower-middle-class milieu. Mr Memory. Gunshot. Hannay and Annabella. Mystery begins.

    B. Hannay's flat
     London. Food, drink, talk. Hannay spends the night with a woman. Two men below on the phone. Hannay helps Annabella. Death of Annabella. Transfer of paranoia. Mystery leads Hannay to Scotland.

II. Scotland
  2. Country
   (day one)

    A. Train to bridge
     Police: 'There's enough evidence there to convict any man'. Forced kiss. Pamela betrays Hannay.

    B. Chase/walk
     (night two)

    C. Crofter's cottage
     Hannay betrayed by host.
     (day two)

    D. Chase
    E. Prof. Jordan's
     Centre of film. Goal of original quest. Jour

ney to Jordan followed by flight from him. Gunshot. DEATH

  3. Small City
   (night three)

    F. Small town. Police. Salvation Army parade. Political rally.

    G. Phoney police
     Forced union: Pamela handcuffed to Hannay.

  4. Country

    H. The moors

    I. Country Inn (see England B)
     Food, drink, talk. Hannay spends the night with a woman. Two men below on the phone. Transfer of paranoia/belief. Hannay protected by host. Pamela helps Hannay. Mystery leads Hannay and Pamela back to England/London.

III. England (night four)
  5. City

    A. Scotland Yard
     Pamela defends Hannay. Police do not believe her story. (see II. A.)

    B. Palladium
     London. Middle-class milieu. Mr Memory. Gunshot. Hannay and Pamela. Voluntary union (see II. Scotland A and G). Mystery resolved.

In fashioning a screenplay out of Somerset Maugham's 'Ashenden' stories (and Campbell Dixon's play), Bennett and Hitchcock made one major change that is illustrative of the sort of bleak, absurdist vision they both share: their secret agents *kill the wrong man* (he is the right man in Maugham)! The guilt that Ashenden and Ilsa feel as a result of this error looks back to that which overwhelms Alice in *Blackmail*, when she anguishes over the fate of Tracy, the blackmailer, who is innocent but presumed guilty of a crime she actually committed. The parallel with Bennett's *Blackmail* continues: Ilsa subsequently prevents Ashenden and 'the General' from killing the real spy, Marvin, much as Alice kept Webber from shooting Tracy.

Having just made *Secret Agent* out of Maugham material, Bennett and Hitchcock then transformed Joseph Conrad's *Secret Agent* into *Sabotage*. Though the change in title was obviously dictated by their prior use of it, the story that Bennett and Hitchcock tell owes as much to their earlier film work together as it does to Conrad's original story. Bennett and Hitchcock invent a love interest for Mrs Verloc, pairing her up with the detective, Ted, who is investigating the activities of her husband, Mr Verloc. In the novel, she kills her husband when he confesses responsibility for the accidental death of her brother Stevie. In the film, Bennett and Hitchcock have her kill her husband partly in self-defence, much as Alice does in *Blackmail*. As in Bennett's play, the policeman, Ted, then shields her of the crime and lets his superiors believe that another man, the Professor, actually committed it. Like Tracy in *Blackmail*, the Professor is followed by the police and dies before he can talk. Ted subsequently prevents Mrs Verloc from confessing her crime. (In Conrad's novel, Mrs Verloc is abandoned by her only ally and commits suicide.)

Prior to leaving England for Hollywood, Bennett worked on the story for *Young and Innocent*, but left before a final script had been prepared. Like *Sabotage*, the film reveals the extent to which the 'typical Hitchcock scenario' had already been devised. Caught between love and duty, a character joins a real criminal or someone-presumed-to-be-a-criminal in outwitting and eluding capture by the police. The familiar love relationship between a policeman and murder suspect is here reversed. The murder suspect is a young man, not a woman, and he is shielded from the police by a

Fig. 4. Poster art for *Secret Agent* (GB, 1936).

young girl who, though not a police officer herself, is the daughter of the local chief constable.

At the heart of *Young and Innocent* lies the couple-on-the-run plot that emerges as a basic structure during the crafting of the script for *The 39 Steps*. Initially distrustful of the hero, the heroine ultimately comes to have faith in him. This is a thematic pattern that has gradually evolved out of the Bennett–Hitchcock collaboration (and will survive it in films such as *Saboteur*).

Yet another feature of the typical plot is the couple's collaborative self-reliance in achieving goals. United by a guilty secret or by knowing 'too much', they cannot go to the police for help but must work together as a couple to solve their problems. Pursued by the police, *Young and Innocent*'s young lovers must track down the real villain themselves before they are caught by the police.

Several years later, when both Bennett and Hitchcock were working in the States, they collaborated for a final time on the script of *Foreign Correspondent* (1940). Though several writers, credited and uncredited, worked on the film, including Ben Hecht, *Foreign Correspondent* was clearly the product of Hitchcock's earlier work with Bennett. The basic narrative pattern is that of *The 39 Steps*, a more or less circular journey. As Matthew Bernstein has observed, the film's hero, Johnnie Jones, resembles Richard Hannay in that his is an 'innocent man drawn into an underworld of espionage'.

> The story's trajectory, which leads Jones to safety and counsel in the home of Stephen Fisher, echoes Hannay's journey to Scotland and the home of spy mastermind Professor Jordan. And the film's MacGuffin that everyone pursues, the paragraph of a peace treaty memorised by the Dutch diplomat Van Meer, was a patent recycling of Mr Memory's knowledge of the *39 Steps*. Even small details, such as Jones's appearance in Carol's hotel bathroom, and their mutual 'kidnapping' in a Cambridge hotel, or the sardonic treatment of official lectures and gatherings ... echo Hannay and Pamela's enforced tryst and Hannay's improvised political speech ... [23]

As in *39 Steps*, the heroine initially rejects the advances of the hero and refuses to believe him (when he tells her of his suspicions about her father).

Pursued by spies, the hero forces himself into the arms of the heroine, who gradually becomes his ally in the pursuit of the missing Van Meer. The script *doubles* the 'typical' love-duty conflict: the hero's duty as a newspaper reporter to get the dirt on Fisher is at odds with his courtship of Fisher's daughter, Carol. Carol's love for her father is set against her loyalty to England. As at the end of *Secret Agent*, the narrative's conflicts find resolution in a spectacular crash (the train in the earlier script becomes a plane), triggered by outside forces beyond the central characters' control.

Over the course of three years (1934–37), Bennett and Hitchcock developed a story formula that, with minor variation, provided Hitchcock with a narrative pattern that would inform much of his subsequent work without Bennett. A study of Bennett's own work for the theatre reveals just how much he brought to this collaboration and how much Hitchcock owed to him.

Bennett's Credits

Produced Plays

> *The Return* (Everyman Theatre, London, 1927; directed by Bennett).
>
> *Blackmail* (Globe Theatre, London, 1928).
>
> *The Last Hour* (Comedy Theatre, London, 1928).
>
> *After Midnight* (Rudolph Steiner, London, 1929; directed by Bennett).
>
> *The Danger Line* (Greenwich, CT., 1929; written with Hazel Marshall).
>
> *Sensation* (Lyceum Theatre, London, 1931; directed by Bennett).
>
> *Big Business* (Beaux-Arts, Monte Carlo, 1932; directed by Bennett).
>
> *Page From a Diary* (aka *Masquerade*, Garrick Theatre, London, 1936).

Screen Credits

> *Blackmail* (BIP, 1929; dir. Hitchcock, based on a play by Bennett).

The Last Hour (Nettlefold, 1930; dir. Walter Forde; based on play by Bennett).

Midnight (Fox, 1931; dir. George King; scenario by Bennett and Billie Bristow, based on Bennett's *After Midnight*).

Number Please (Fox, 1931; dir. George King; screenplay by Bennett and Billie Bristow).

Deadlock (King, 1931; dir. King; story by Bennett and Bristow).

Two Way Street (Nettlefold, 1931; dir. King; story by Bennett and Bristow).

Partners Please (PPC, 1932; dir. Lloyd Richards; story by Bennett).

Matinee Idol (Wyndham, 1933; dir. George A. Cooper; story by Bennett).

Hawleys of High Street (BIP, 1933; dir. Thomas Bentley; sc. by Bennett, Syd Courtenay, and Frank Launder, based on the play by Walter Ellis).

Paris Plane (Sound City/MGM, 1933; dir. J.P. Carstairs; story by Bennett).

Mannequin (Real Arts, 1933; dir. George A. Cooper; story by Bennett).

The House of Trent (B&H, 1933; dir. Norman Walker; story by Bennett and Bristow).

Gay Love (British Lion, 1934; dir. Leslie Hiscott; sc. by Bennett and Bristow, b/o play by Audrey and Waveney Carton).

Secret of the Loch (Wyndham, 1934; dir. Milton Rosmer; story by Bennett and Bristow).

The Man Who Knew Too Much (Gaumont, 1934; dir. Hitchcock; sc. by Bennett, A.R. Rawlinson, and Edwin Greenwood, b/o story by Bennett and D.B. Wyndham Lewis.

Night Mail (British Lion, 1935; dir. Herbert Smith; story by Bennett and Bristow).

The Clairvoyant (Gainsborough, 1935; dir. Maurice Elvey; sc. by Bennett, Bryan Edgar Wallace and Robert Edmunds).

Blue Smoke (Fox-British, 1935; dir. Ralph Ince; sc. by Fenn Aherie and Ingram d'Abbes, b/o story by Bennett).

The 39 Steps (Gaumont, 1935; dir. Hitchcock; sc. by Bennett and Alma Reville, b/o novel by John Buchan).

King of the Damned (Gaumont, 1936; dir. Walter Forde; sc. by Bennett and A.R. Rawlinson, b/o play by John Chancellor).

The Secret Agent (Gaumont, 1936; dir. Hitchcock; sc. by Bennett; b/o play by Campbell Dixon and stories by Somerset Maugham).

Sabotage (Gaumont, 1936; dir. Hitchcock; sc. by Bennett, b/o novel by Joseph Conrad).

King Soloman's Mines (Gaumont, 1937; dir. Robert Stevenson; sc. by Bennett and Stevenson).

Young and Innocent (Gainsborough/Gaumont, 1937; dir. Hitchcock; sc. by Bennett and Alma Reville, b/o novel by Josephine Tey).

The Young in Heart (Selznick/UA, 1938; dir. Richard Wallace; sc. by Paul Osborn and Bennett, b/o story by I.A.R. Wylie).

Balalaika (MGM, 1939; dir. Reinhold Schunzel; sc. by Leon Gordon, Bennett, and Jacques Duval from any operetta by Eric Maschwitz).

Foreign Correspondent (Wanger/UA, 1940; dir. Hitchcock; sc. by Bennett and Joan Harrison, b/o book by Vincent Sheehan).

They Dare Not love (Columbia, 1941; dir. James Whale; sc. by Bennett and Ernest Vajda, b/o story by James Edward Grant).

Joan of Paris (RKO, 1942; dir. Robert Stevenson; sc. by Bennett and Ellis St. Joseph, b/o story by Jacques Thery and Georges Kessel).

Reap the Wild Wind (Paramount, 1942; dir Cecil B. DeMille; sc. by Alan LeMay, Bennett, and Jesse Lasky, Jr.).

Forever and a Day (RKO, 1943; dir. Clair, Goulding, Hardwicke, Lloyd, Saville, Stevenson and Wilcox; sc. by Bennett, C.S. Forester, Christopher Isherwood and D. Stewart).

The Story of Dr. Wassell (Paramount, 1944; dir. DeMille; sc. by Alan LeMay and Bennett).

Unconquered (Paramount, 1947; dir. DeMille; sc. by Bennett, Fredric M. Frank and Jesse Lasky, Jr., b/o novel by Neil H. Swanson).

Ivy (Universal, 1947; dir. Sam Wood; sc. by Bennett, b/o novel by Marie Belloc Lowndes).

The Sign of the Ram (Columbia, 1948; dir. John Sturges; sc. by Bennett, b/o novel by Margaret Ferguson).

Black Magic (UA, 1949); dir. Gregory Ratoff; sc. by Bennett, b/o novel by Alexandre Dumas).

Madness of the Heart (Universal, 1950; dir. Bennett; sc. by Bennett, b/o novel by Flora Sandstrom).

Where Danger Lives (RKO, 1950; dir. John Farrow; sc. by Bennett. b/o story by Leo Rosten).

Kind Lady (MGM, 1951; dir. John Sturges; sc. by Jerry Davis, Edward Chodorov and Bennett, b/o story by Hugh Walpole).

The Green Glove (UA, 1953; dir. Rudolph Mate; story and sc. by Bennett).

No Escape (UA, 1953; dir. and sc. by Bennett).

Dangerous Mission (RKO, 1954; dir. Louis King; sc. by Bennett).

Phenix City Story (Allied Artists, 1955; dir. Phil Karlson; sc. by Daniel Mainwaring and Bennett, uncredited).

The Man Who Knew Too Much (Paramount, 1956; dir. Hitchcock; sc. by John Michael Hayes and Angus McPhail, b/o story by Bennett and D.B. Wyndham Lewis).

Curse of the Demon (a.k.a. *Night of the Demon*, Columbia, 1957; dir. Jacques Tourneur; sc. by Bennett and Hal E. Chester, b/o story by Montagu R. James).

The Story of Mankind (Warner Bros., 1957; dir. Irwin Allen; sc. by Allen and Bennett, b/o book by Hendrik Willem Van Loon).

The Big Circus (Allied Artists, 1959; dir. Joseph M. Newman; sc. by Bennett, Allen, and Irving Wallace, b/o story by Allen).

The Lost World (Fox, 1960; dir. Allen; sc. by Allen and Bennett, b/o novel by Sir Arthur Conan Doyle).

Voyage to the Bottom of the Sea (Fox, 1961; dir. Allen; sc. by Allen and Bennett, b/o story by Allen).

Five Weeks in a Balloon (Fox, 1962; dir. Allen; sc. by Bennett, Allen, and Albert Gail, b/o story by Jules Verne).

War Gods of the Deep (American-International, 1965; dir. Jacques Tourneur; sc. by Bennett and Louis M. Heyward, b/o poem and story by Edgar Allan Poe).

Charles Bennett was one of the first Hollywood screenwriters to write for television. He wrote over 150 hour-and-a-half shows for Fox, Warners, Four Star, Screen Gems, Schlitz Playhouse, Fireside Theater, TPA, Cavalcade of America, The Christophers, and Lux Theater. In the mid-1950s, he directed (for producer Edward Small) the *Monte Cristo* television series and *The New Adventures of Charlie Chan*. In 1958, he won the Christopher Award for best television direction of the year for 'The Gift of Dr. Minot' in the *Cavalcade of America* series. For Promesa Films in Mexico, he directed two feature films – *Prince of the Church* and *The Cardinal*.

Notes

1.   Hitchcock's work cannot be reduced to one or even two typical story patterns. However, one of the most successful and frequently used scenario types associated with Hitchcock is that which Hitchcock developed with Bennett.

2.   Charles Bennett, interview with the author (21 March 1978).

3.   The film was to be set in Washington, DC. The murder victim was to be patterned after Donald Trump.

4.   *Daily Variety* (3 March 1995): 5.

5.   Letter from Bennett to the author, dated 6 August 1979. Bennett shared his cameo in *The 39 Steps*

with director Alfred Hitchcock. Bennett and Hitchcock appear outside the Music Hall, walking side by side, as Hannay and Anabella Smith board a bus.

6. 'Short Biography and Major Writing Credits' for Charles Bennett, provided to the author by Mr Bennett.

7. Peggy Ashcroft, who later stars in *The 39 Steps,* appeared as the hero's love interest, Mary Dunn, on stage in *The Return.*

8. *The Return* (London: Ernest Benn Ltd, 1928),

9. Hitchcock, 'Direction', *Footnotes to the Film,* ed. Charles Davy (London: Lovat Dickson Ltd): 13.

10. Hitchcock, 'Direction', in *Footnotes to the Film,* ed. Davy: 3–5.

11. *Blackmail.* London: Rich & Cowan Ltd (1934): 26.

12. *Blackmail,* 56.

13. *Blackmail,* 67.

14. *Blackmail,* 92.

15. *Blackmail,* 97.

16. The wreck is caused by the British airforce, which drops bombs on the train.

17. Bennett, interview with the author.

18. Charles Bennett, *The Last Hour* (London: Rich and Cowan Ltd, 1934): 35.

19. Letter to the author, dated 27 January 1980.

20. *The Danger Line,* 2–7.

21. Quoted in James Naremore, *Filmguide to Psycho* (Bloomington: Indiana University Press, 1973): 11.

22. Author's interview with Bennett in Los Angeles on 21 March 1978.

23. Matthew Bernstein, *Walter Wanger: Hollywood Independent* (Berkeley: University of California Press, 1994): 159.

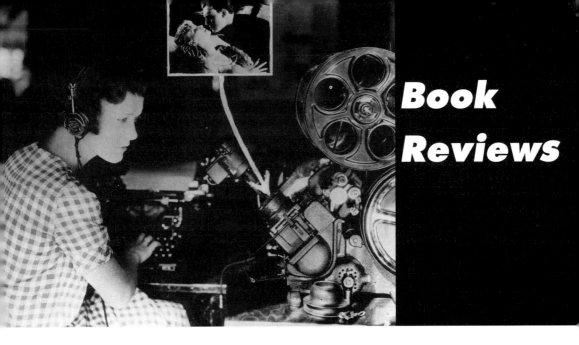

Book Reviews

Without lying down: Frances Marion and the powerful women of early Hollywood. Cari Beauchamp. (Scribner: New York, 1997), $30.

John Belton

n a 1986 book dealing with American screen-writers, *Backstory: Interviews with Screenwriters of Hollywood's Golden Age*, Pat McGilligan notes that 'before 1926, at least to judge from the official credits, there were no screenwriters'. He goes on to explain that there were 'gag-writers, continuity writers, treatment writers, scenarists, adapters, titlists, what-have-you'. In part, McGilligan wants to distinguish the screenwriting practices for silent films from those of the sound film era, but his elision of the development of screenwriting in the silent era is symptomatic of the ways in which the history of screenwriting has been written. It is the craft of word-smiths and begins with the sound film; the 30 years of cinema prior to the sound film emerged miraculously from the head of Zeus without the intermediating presence of the screenwriter.

What is also revealing about McGilligan's book is that thirteen of the fourteen screenwriters interviewed are male (among the thirteen is the team of Frances Goodrich and Albert Hackett).

To some extent, McGilligan's percentages re-flect the state of screenwriting in the sound era when male writers, including successful novelists, playwrights, and poets, dominated the craft. But, as Cari Beauchamp reports in *Without Lying Down: Frances Marion and the Powerful Women of Early Hollywood*, half of all films written between 1912 and 1925 were written by women. According to screenwriter Frances Marion, with the coming of sound 'the general opinion was that women were not capable of overcoming the new and compli-cated technique'. Marion, whose two Oscars were won for early sound film scripts, *The Big House* (MGM, 1930) and *The Champ* (MGM, 1931), pro-vides evidence to the contrary.

Beauchamp's book seeks to fill in the gaps that exist in mainstream accounts of Hollywood screen-writing. Scholarly work on silent cinema, such as that of Anthony Slide, Kevin Brownlow and others, has acknowledged the importance of women writers and directors, but this work has not been acknowledged by trade-press writers prior to Beau-champ (whose book is published by Scribners).

There is clearly a polemical thrust to Beau-champ's biography of Marion and other 'powerful women'. That is why her focus is not just on the

Fig. 1. Mary Pickford and her favourite screenwriter, Frances Marion [photo courtesy of Scribner].

career of Frances Marion but on a group of female writers and stars whose careers depended upon a network of mutual support and assistance. To some extent, Beauchamp provides a new model for understanding Hollywood: in her book it emerges as a system of social connections. History is not driven exclusively by economics or technology, but by an ideology of social relations, that is, by who knows whom. Beauchamp's presentation of this 'social history' is not very sophisticated. Her interests, after all, are not driven by an attempt to revolutionise the paradigms that dominate the writing of film history; she just wants to tell Frances Marion's story. The character she constructs emerges as a figure who understood the power structure of the studio system and who learned how to develop a certain agency within it.

One could write a history of Hollywood around Frances Marion. She began writing for motion pictures in 1915; she worked as a writer/story editor in Hollywood until 1946; her career spans the development of classical Hollywood cinema from five-

reelers to two-hour features, from silent to sound films, and from small production companies to giant studios such as MGM. She was credited with the writing of over 325 scripts. Her career began in 1914 when she worked at Bosworth for director Lois Weber.

Beauchamp repeats the famous story of Marion's first writing assignment. Extras on Weber's pictures were occasionally required to appear to speak. They initially adlibbed their lines. But lip-readers in the audiences could read these lines and complained about their irrelevance to the story. As a result of these complaints, Weber asked Marion to write relevant dialogue for these extras – and to direct them, while appearing on-screen as an extra herself.

Later Marion wrote at least eighteen scripts for Mary Pickford, as well as several films for Clara Kimball Young, Alice Brady, Marie Dressler, Marion Davies, Elsie Janis, Alma Rubens, Norma Talmadge, Lillian Gish, Greta Garbo, Jean Harlow and other top stars. She worked on numerous films for directors Frank Borzage and George W. Hill. She was a favourite of producers William Randolph Hearst and Irving Thalberg. She won two Academy Awards and she was one of the highest paid screenwriters in Hollywood, earning as much as $3000 a week (from Sam Goldwyn in 1928). Among her credits are scripts for *The Poor Little Rich Girl* (1917), *Rebecca of Sunnybrook Farm* (1917), *Humoresque* (1920), *Secrets* (1924, 1933), *Lazybones* (1925), *Stella Dallas* (1925), *The Son of the Sheik* (1926), *The Scarlet Letter* (1926), *The Winning of Barbara Worth* (1926), *Love* (1927), *The Wind* (1928), *Anna Christie* (1930), *Min and Bill* (1930), *Dinner at Eight* (1933) and *Camille* (1937).

Beauchamp views Marion's career in terms of sexual politics. Marion gets her start because of the help of female friends, such as Dressler, Weber and Pickford. Lecherous male producers, ranging from William Fox to Louis B. Mayer (who pinched her rear end when he first hired her to write a script), reduce her to a sexual object. 'Woman Against the Sea', a story she had written about an independent woman who becomes the captain of a ship and puts down a potential mutiny, was rewritten for William Farnum and re-titled *The Iron Man*. *The Scarlet Letter* languished as a project at MGM because the studio's screenwriters tried to tell the story from Rev. Dimmesdale's point of view. Marion made the script work by turning it into Hester Prynne's story, a shift that seems quite obvious in retrospect but which was apparently inconceivable prior to Marion's 'feminist' intervention.

Marion 'tended to be so loyal to her woman friends that she didn't trust the men they were with'. Thus Doug Fairbanks is seen as a jealous and possessive husband. John Emerson was 'a total dullard with a "constipated brain" who manipulated Anita [Loos]'.

Marion emerges from Beauchamp's biography as a 'New Woman', as a modern, independent, sexually active, career woman who delighted in violating the rigid conventions that men had established for female behaviour. Thus she is the first woman to win two Academy Awards for screenwriting, the first Allied woman to cross the Rhine after World War I, and the first vice-president and only woman board member of the Writer's Guild. But, during the sound era (and especially after Thalberg's death in 1936), she was forced into a certain anonymity. She notes that 'Bess Meredith, Anita Loos, and I were asked our advice on virtually every script MGM produced in the thirties' but they were forced to 'carry the scripts in "unmarked plain covers" because they were painfully aware of the whispers about "the tyranny of the women writers"'. Yet Marion refused to 'lie down'. She continued to write, to paint, to sculpt, and to create, until her death in 1973.

Beauchamp's book is extensively researched, drawing on interviews with Marion's family and friends; on Marion's personal papers, unpublished manuscripts, and appointment books; on files at the Academy of Motion Picture Arts and Sciences, at USC, at the Museum of Modern Art, and at the Library of Congress; on MGM contracts and files held by Turner Broadcasting; and on scholars of silent cinema, such as Kevin Brownlow, David Gill, Richard Koszarski, David Shepard and Anthony Slide. It contains a filmography, listing Marion's works, a bibliography, and it has an index. It is extensively annotated.

The writing is a bit programmatic – the introduction of each new personality is accompanied by a requisite family biography. There is considerable name-dropping: every celebrity Marion ever met – from Rachmaninoff to George Gershwin – receives mention. And the individual chapters of the biography lack focus: thus the chapter on sound shifts (without much sense) to the morality clauses in actors' contracts; to abortions, homosexuality, and drugs; and then to happily married couples, such as Marion and Fred Thompson or Irving Thalberg and Norma Shearer. Nonetheless, the book serves as a valuable complement to Marion's somewhat self-censored, earlier biography, *Off With Their Heads* (1972). ♠

FILM HISTORY

Back issue and subscription order form

PLEASE SUPPLY:

.... Subscription(s) to *Film History*
at Institutional/Private rate (please specify)
Surface/Airmail (please specify)
.... Back issues of the following volumes/issues
....
....
I enclose payment of AUD$/US$ ....
Please send me a Pro-forma invoice for:
AUD$/US$ ....
Please debit my Access/Master Card/Visa/
American Express/Diner's Club credit card:
Account no...Expiry.........
Name ....
Address ....
....
....
.... Zip/Postcode ....

Signature ....Date ....
(This form may be photocopied)

SUBSCRIPTION RATES & BACK ISSUE PRICES

Institutional Subscription rates:
   All countries (except N. America)
   Surface mail   AUD$172
   Airmail   AUD$194
   N. America
   Surface mail   US$151   Airmail   US$172
Private Subscription rates (subscribers warrant that copies are for their PERSONAL use only):
   All countries (except N. America)
   Surface mail   AUD$66
   Airmail   AUD$88
   N. America
   Surface mail   US$59   Airmail   US$79
Back issues: All issues available – Volumes 1 to 9:
US$20/AUD$24 each number.

JOHN LIBBEY & COMPANY PTY LTD,
Level 10, 15–17 Young Street
Sydney, NSW 2000, Australia
Telephone: +61 (0)2 9251 4099
Fax: +61 (0)2 9251 4428
E-mail: jlsydney@mpx.com.au

FILM HISTORY

An International Journal

Aims and Scope

The subject of *Film History* is the historical development of the motion picture, and the social, technological and economic context in which this has occurred. Its areas of interest range from the technical and entrepreneurial innovations of early and pre-cinema experiments, through all aspects of the production, distribution, exhibition and reception of commercial and non-commercial motion pictures.
In addition to original research in these areas, the journal will survey the paper and film holdings of archives and libraries worldwide, publish selected examples of primary documentation (such as early film scenarios) and report on current publications, exhibitions, conferences and research in progress. Many future issues will be devoted to comprehensive studies of single themes.

Instructions to Authors

Manuscripts will be accepted with the understanding that their content is unpublished and is not being submitted for publication elsewhere. If any part of the paper has been previously published, or is to be published elsewhere, the author must include this information at the time of submittal. Manuscripts should be sent to the Editor-in-Chief:

   Richard Koszarski
   Box Ten
   Teaneck, NJ 07666, USA
   E-mail: filmhist@aol.com
excepting for submissions to thematic issues directed by one of the Associate Editors.

The publishers will do everything possible to ensure prompt publication, therefore it is required that each submitted manuscript be in complete form. Please take the time to check all references, figures, tables and text for errors before submission.
Form: Authors are requested to submit their manuscripts on diskette – IBM format (preferably).